The Melancholy Of A Life
As The Joy Of Living It Slowly Chills

Poems

Philip Ramp

Fomite
Burlington, Vermont

Copyright 2018 © Philip Ramp

All rights reserved. No part of this book may be reproduced in any form or by any means without the prior written consent of the publisher, except in the case of brief quotations used in reviews and certain other noncommercial uses permitted by copyright law.

ISBN-13: 978-1-944388-54-6
Library of Congress Control Number: requested

Fomite
58 Peru Street
Burlington, VT 05401
www.fomitepress.com

To Sarah, as always…without your love joy would have remained a mystery rather than a revelation, but since your death, and though I was born in a cold land, I found I'm only now beginning to learn the meaning of chill.

Contents

Trying, Yet Again, To Put It Better Than...	1
Stones Firm Up Roots So Grass...	8
Hot Morning, Standing Between Sprinklers	14
On Letting Tomorrow Wrap Tomorrow	20
If "Nearly" Were To Prove A Password...	23
On Butterflies, Mandlebrot And Silver Lining Departments	27
So Where Is The Who, And Who Cares?	32
Time, Time, Time...	39
Temporarily Untitled (Till He Finds The Fit For His Life Therein)	46
An Embrace	50
Starting With A Leaf And A River	52
On Interpretation Of Patterns And Being...Circumspect	56
On How Things Are Stacked	60
Cold Probability Or Warm Mystery?	64
The Sensation Was Of Sinking Without Going Down	68
None Of What He Was Given Will Ever Be His Even Once, Let Alone Again	74
A Valley, A Village, And Pretty Much Take It From There	79
A Dance Best Attempted By Those Long Experienced At Being Amateurs	84
From A Distance Mistakes Can Often Be Mistaken For Right Ways	87
Detachment Or An Active Solitude?	92
The Trick Is To Get There Just As It's Turning Away And In Such A Manner You Can Be Sure It Won't Turn Back	96
Long Ago: Such A Strange Aesthetic!	102
On Despair Setting Off On A New Course	106
Pull The Other One	111
There Have To Be Places Where No One's To Blame	117
Who Can He Trust To Keep An Eye On His Hovering Breath?	122

Trying, Yet Again, To Put It Better Than...

And by "better than" he means thinking through more
carefully (that is thinking, not guessing)
the...over part, and because it's so much larger,
so... over, choosing a specific place to start:

how the wedding ring has come to hold only that
one finger's voice, or why
each wind's voice can now spring loose
only single things and leaving
them up in the air -- though not for all that long.

But without such vigilance (he's learned
by instinct – a field not nearly enough research has
been done in...) things lose even the sense he

made of them when he thought getting them
done quickly would do, and if his
heart then goes out to them as unprepared too, it
may be the last thing he hears from it, too.

And that's just the start. It could well mean the goose
he's chasing here will no longer be wild,
not worth even a gander, and perhaps not
even in evidence when he needs to produce it –
by the time he reaches the end of this poem that is!

What he means is, he's been watching birds making
cloud pies and when he looks away
he knows, by the feel of his limbs, he's
closer to being that stick-figure again,

the one he so felt like as a child,
though his shadow's filled out since then.

The question surrounding, if loosely, the nature of then,
remains: what's the good of experience if
it's less help to coping, let alone understanding or wisdom..
than innocence? That is he feels he needs to go

deeper, and even though he's already in so deep
he'll never get out, it's only age there's always an out...

not yet! at odder angles then, making depth linear or
so complex one's ups and downs are
as breathtaking as the climbing of...
and then come immediately crashing down
a mountain but all converted to an incredible length!

Giving him time –and what's deeper than that?
to convert the most stubborn silences
into malleable, congenial and oh
so willing words, hoping somehow, in this
way, to drain the last drop of meaning from them before...

before later of course! but does he really want to
run them dry, treat them like wells
that is – and while knowing
we shouldn't be treating them that way?

So forget the title, he's not trying, though yet again
fits, but is only buying time to come up
with some kind of theme; and now he must concentrate,
(should have listened to instinct and
made a habit of this) set the scene as it were,

no is, right now!: morning, elastic and inconclusive,
glass-darkly size, taking the shape of a
peopled city, though finding it harder
and harder to...people it – and much the same

as getting meaning out of words (they're not
much more than stick-figures themselves
he now realizes; though they pretend to
swagger, while merely staggering about, stepping
in front of cars, wandering off for a coffee

and winding up with a one-way ticket to the stars:
and not for a game of pick-up-stardust-sticks
either!); for words, it seems, are far more
versatile at even the most extreme
sports than bodies could ever be or hope to,

even in their wildest dreams (which are children of
despair rather than hope as one should by
now know, after all who gave them birth!)

He imagines a third rail sizzle as the horizon sparks
into life and wonders if he might die
touching it but... without having the needed reach...

well, by the time he's dead-ended his way through
that this "rail" has led him down by
the now abandoned tracks, where
clones of Diogenes, and even though they may
only live in cardboard shacks,
still dream of their own barrel one day; but for now,

no more than distant relatives of his, lacking
his feel for the ferment inside.

(It's pitiful but, as he sees it, his only hope of getting
himself back, the worse for wear...perhaps...
who's he kidding the worse for not being worn...)

On a more, make that less, abstract level, each new
increment of light seems to exponentially
expand the space it occupies, as if making room
for the dark swarms of people already
wound up and sent off with a spin, to full,
and highly precarious, tilt status: that is, nearly all

their space is being consumed in supposedly maintaining
an equilibrium that cannot be even, or ever,

attained except in the fantasy world of chaos-juggling
words – so he would now only hope he could
keep his private distance,
the one, and only, part of his birthright
that should be left...how can he be sure...
it's too early for...anything he can imagine... yet,

one that might accommodate such old and incomplete
agonies that memory keeps nagging
him to complete,
acting as if he were hiding something
from it (when it's the one does the hiding,

it's the one that chooses to forget!) better then to wait
and at that exact distance he's trying to maintain,
until, anyway, he feels sure enough

of the rhythm (it won't be Bach
probably, but a fugue state is not only possible

but would prove he'd adhered to the rules of
composition, no matter how bizarrely
the harmonies fit) and only move in then,
secure himself to the flow, feel the strength,

the pull of the massive unawareness within
him and carried along on that mindless
surge he should, again, be able
to watch the sky come down, wait for
him at river's end –like the destiny
he once imagined at the other end of himself....

his stick-figure finally doing what it was meant
to do: float! Simple as a Feynman diagram;
he clearly knew all about stick-figures too, not
only their strengths but the lengths to which they would go.

Bringing him to a stop, not to, or by, himself, but rather
at "Old Unfaithful", the Dali-inspired, kaleidoscopically
lurid timepiece, some famous sculptor
suckered the powers-that-were into placing across
from City Hall, where it audibly and erratically,

flashes "seconds" in Day-Glo like lumps, a marvel
they say everyone says (though he's yet to
hear anyone saying that except
perhaps in the *%!@# patois found in Marvel comics)

and he admits it is a marvel that any time
can be told like this, even though it's

not the one on which the city or anything else
for that matter… runs, or is supposed to –
maybe the sculptor was not so much fulfilling
a commission as making a point?

A derelict appears like…clockwork (don't knock
coincidence it works better than accident!)
and salutes the "clock" with his bottle,
tipping it up steadily, like the second hand on
an actual clock. A cabbie drifts by telling
the world to go fuck itself. It complies.

Whoop of a siren and he's spilled out (still thinking,
still not over… over… yet) with the other
overflow from the dark swarming
crowd and finds himself finally stranded on
the other side, glad to see his anonymity,

at least, is still intact after the impact-cracks caused by
today's vicissitudes. It's a street where only
money is made so if one's not into money
there's no need, no place, to stay. But he's on
the "other side" so he's already strayed…anyway…

for some reason, he can still remember it is (was)
the street he first noticed no one was
noticing him; that is, he must have been…
visible but no one reacted and perhaps it was just as

well, for sticking to memory, (trusting it not to
for once come unglued) he made his way…
(the one he got lost on once but still…
he does know the way!) otherwise it would have been

impossible for him, he's certain, to get... through.
But he is through with that for now and feeling
much like the snow waste from a recent
storm, still piled high along the curbs looking like

the insides of patients who didn't make it, didn't get...
through... often after degenerate but perhaps
not unhappy lives...he hears a mechanical chirp
he places somewhere inside but then decides it

must be the DON'T CROSS sign. His stick figure...still
capable of warning him: be on the alert!
Things change, things stay the same, but in
between is the place one had better have something
special to say for oneself and this time put it better than...

Stones Firm Up Roots So Grass…

In the vestibule of evening the sun lies like a pebble,
but so highly polished it seems
as if it's being prepared to be the unique,
and official, jewel in the crown of

the local demigod. Nijinsky disguised as a spiraling
cirrus levitating so long the sky goes
into what could be a hypnotic sleep – (suggestible…
if he only knew some sky words!)

before, anyway, his dreams are ready to counter
sleep's nightly assaults of
emptiness, leaving him at a loss for
a word or a note that would fill the metaphysical

gap in his awe of them as separate but equal worlds.

Something so clearly imagined it will be able to
move essence from a commonplace
abstract plane to the edge dividing the finite
from infinite – they have to be
separate, but the line being on the extreme
end of the invisible, even God must feel His way.

Perhaps, then, waking is life's strangest dream,
at least giving one the illusion of
walking through a magical façade and
reclaiming the world (merely a similitude, he suspects –

otherwise, why did waking need illusions at

all, that's sleep's preserve, isn't it?)

He'll have to leave it to light yet again, that grand
ventriloquist of all the voices of space,
and even greater illusionist, being
able to pretend it's drawing them out of
the earth, then has everyone, everything, speaking
at once though everyone would swear
the voice was his! And everything as vociferously denying it!

Then again he sometimes thinks dreams are more
like ankles (surprise!), as both are so...
complex and fragile they shouldn't work
at all and yet both are able to
withstand enormous stress – or fracture at the slightest tap.

His waking, all too often of late, to the sound of his
dreams beginning to crack in God's fat hard-
squeezing-never-more-pain-than-you-can-bear hand.

No wonder when he returns at the end of the
day he changes immediately, showing
he knows when to give up the pretense of being awake.

Focus or hocus-pocus the self poses as the locus of
even the most elusive shadows, trying to
avoid the ruckus of thought, its rictus
smile when it puns – more than enough to
make him want to attend to the green light of
dawn, share the same thrill as love at
first sight linking the ands, buts and maybes

and while the colors proceed to lay claim to, (and then

find themselves being dispossessed of, before
even submitting their claim), morning's
variable part in what could be nothing else but
never definably is... a day. Not a Rubik cube solution

or a re-enactment of receiving a map of the future
from a benevolent muse or even a snake
learned in the ways of Eve celebrating
their anniversary, one he so wants so needs
to attend but how can he when he's on
a path others made, while adding, he hopes, his own

perspective on things and in much the same way a spring
leaf graphically describes what happened
during the night, dropping the same
eager shadows at irregular intervals, as hints.

(and he's not longing for paths not taken either; all
have been or they wouldn't exist and
yet no one has ever admitted to being on one –forget
it, better to take an untaken deep breath!)

No, it's more like looking at a stretch of water as if
it were a transcript and wondering if it's
ever needed to be revised, for
neither experience nor understanding come
into this and even if they did, could
never tell us if the mind is friend or foe: heart
to heart as far as it goes – if it knows
the way and if the vessels are reliable, and...anyway

to get back to where he should have started, what
the title stated that must be explained...

it's complicated...so stones do firm
up roots so grass will have the strength to
move those same stones aside.

Should be enough, he thinks, to convince one that
if he squeezes stone as hard as he can
it will emit a faint light, without showing
a visible crack. A light that will put in perspective

the distance between daily here and the sheer
poetic delirium on which the imagination gorges itself

to meet the demands of furiously composing hands,
themselves distracted by senses gone manic,
so that ultimately a vital part of us
is absent from what we create and it is

in this fevered dark the grand blooms naturally
choose to hide; stay hidden too. Like
God's creations will only reveal themselves
to belief, if you can believe that, well...

Now moving on to rooftops in the distance –
so brilliant with overlapping and
spectral spectrums of colors they cry out
for a more advanced form of eye
and the sky's sparkling blue jewel tarnishes
the luster of the demigod's crown as he slips away
with his throne into the dark.

The coffee now dregs, but after that he's able to drink
it anyway, the book nearly read so he reads
it backward for a while, his eyes

blurred from too many coffee dregs,
too many reverse words, (one really enough)

automatically turning toward the peculiar and equally
blurred shine off the river that appears this
time of year, grass and flowers similarly
smudged by the winds flowing toward
them, all of them, what the hell, rivers themselves!

As light leaves the day it's as if everything else
connected to it is also trying to get away,
but like the water, like all flow, the essence
remains: this ceaseless moving is what makes it, itself.

And so even the flow is not what it was, but not
as a poem changes each time it's read,
(don't try for backward: it won't accept) or
as thoughts and grass can lift great
weights, while remaining almost weightless themselves –

for unlike flow, they are, like us, quickly spent, our
rhythm and luminance absorbed by that one
paramount moment of time, set aside till
we're inside it, where it's impossible to tell what's

living from what's dying, and they're not only not the
same, but there is a third stage as well,
finding gravitational waves so it won't be long….

waves that should, as gravity ultimately does have its
way, carry us past stages, past the stones,
the roots and the grass and, it
would also seem, perhaps past flow itself.

Hot Morning, Standing Between Sprinklers

Eyes open but seeing nothing, so near, and yet so not
here, so…agoraphobic if one looks too long,
not like a chasm but not unlike
one either – he remembers the…sensation

early, maybe clearer in the absence of sight – the way
they leaned over those chasms, so terrifyingly
attractive, like promises hidden in
hope – as if they were babies in cribs, who, having

pulled themselves up to their first height, immediately look
straight into the abyss – and coo, no, cry
out in delight! feeling the unique
buoyancy of being touched all over by
not much of anything; when true
love makes its only, irrevocably private, point.
....
By then having completed the rituals of waking and traversed
the convoluted passageway that led him
out of sleep, he was up, if not up for it, pausing –
though since he's just started up and down
still hasn't chosen a place…anyway, trying to absorb

the mood of the hot morning as it stood between sprinklers,
taking its rainbow bath, enjoying especially
what seemed to be the spectrum's
ironically enigmatic laugh. In the way a child
(not a baby, having grown since his always premature

birth at dawn!) toddles slowly through gathering colors

only to find on the other side, that last
year's hill of lawn is now though equally lush,
quite flat, is barely running up or
down at all, where before it was steep and fast.

Time, for these moments, so precariously balanced
between making us believe things go from
greater to lesser while at the same time insisting the
volume of less is the most capacious of all!
....
Later, preferably not too late, another day, another…anyway,
all night the moon cruised between clouds
crooning medleys of lullabies that might have been
coaxed from the lonely, unloved Rock
of Ages over the eons, ones he so yearned to listen to

but night wouldn't give in and by exerting itself
excessively, finally sweated his sleep
out of those clouds and it felt like it – dreams
not nearly so moonstruck as they appeared –
let him leave it at that – except…they
reworked the clouds till the moon came back from exile –
dreams! Gotta love 'em. Or else.

But now noon's (see how much he misses without missing
it – and he expects respect?) incandescent feline
purr insinuates itself like a votive
offering between the shimmering ruins of trees.
Feels good, feels bad, who knows, feels

is what's needed, no matter what kind, for all the while
the stones on the hills are throbbing like
terrible tumors -- but ones that will never burst.

Just imagine the feeling inherent in that! No love here,
only fate, though somehow they share a deeper
privacy than that, and not by mistake.
　　　　　………………………………………
Figures waver and pass like alien Brancusian forms, and as
if meditating using their memories for orientation
for the present has yet to find a direction –
when art itself will become a form of meditation, not

a portrayal, but an immersion, a surface folded, so as to
include every eventuality, assuming without
question it hadn't happened -- yet,
or if it had, hadn't been used up… yet.

No distance is reliable, yet one must trust to a… certain degree
of separation, insist on it – assuming one
still wants to exist, for there is always doubt…

actually there isn't, just the sense of insecurity when one
can't use to one's advantage what
the windhover does, did anyway when Hopkins
had it… he means, needing to contend
with his despair it's a miracle it ever flew again!
Hopkins' point, he supposes… anyway…

Fortunately while he's able to keep Hopkins in mind thinking
all this, the bird can't, ergo flies off.
So, it's never a stand-off between alternatives
but there's too much between here
and there for them to ever develop close
relations let alone an affair.

And in fact it's cool – just how long ago was the heat
the birds are chattering about so casually
in the language of now (makes our
language look like a backward step,
evolutionarily anyway). Just a breeze he soon learns,
the birds had it right all along.

But they don't get to choose, to tell in so many words
(and many they are!) choose whether it
was or will be, a Father Knows Best canned
laughter heat or a real no holds barred heat that will

still fit a memory and yet be able to pull it tight as the present,
not a wrinkle or hint of one, letting them
know they can store it in time but
that space is its element? Either or…or…or…?

Or (there's always room for one more, like beer), and more
metaphysically, (outside time, there's always
the potential anyway for more of it – enough! no more
more!) a momentary lull in dimensions,
spread in this singular air like… an orchid's roots,

tingling with the nourishment drawn from that nothingness
he saw on waking, pretending now it's but air?

In any case, never telling him, or anyone, but implying,
that all these lives and their dreams have never
been used properly, nor have they ever even learned
anything of how they, far more amazing than
any orchid, go about so radically transforming nothingness

into air –but isn't the real question whether nothing is even ever there when no one is there to not observe it?

Will inertia and gravity alone keep the turbines of thought
turning though the power steadily declines as
the lake behind the dam begins to leak through, no
immediate danger except a psychological one,
perhaps —eventually revealing the village anyway,
that once seemed built at the center of all time –

and what happened to those living there when time stopped?
And how will the survivors, learning for the
first time that's what they are, deal with
their inundated past they knew nothing of, being fully exposed?

Or will the dam burst and sweep away the last pretenses
to an identity, a profusion of arrhythmic rainbows
roaring down a gorge like a huge mutant
kaleidoscope -- "it's enough to make one wanna cry!"

It's like waiting for the dead to come back with all their
suppressed demands and finding to their horror
it's not in their hands, and then, considered more closely,
finding it is again -- to their delight!

For then they can look at the dam deep in the gorge as if
it were holding not merely the water but
the whole mountain back. And not give a damn
when everything in sight is buried in water and stone –

and just like they are – right is right! It would be like that though
dead things remained the source of that delight!

....

18

The sprinklers shut off and descend into the other earth
they've so lovingly prepared, without ever
revealing why they need to be so circumspectly,
yet precisely engineered. The last of that mist falling
round him, and watching it thin, clear, the design
of these moments' waterfall reenters the sky
and the village, safely under the water again, breathes a sigh.

On Letting Tomorrow Wrap Tomorrow

His coat is thinner so he puts it on earlier, leaves the future
as a ruse of memory for now. Lets, that is, experience stay
fluid, so no moment can use "same-old" as a crutch; one

a deflating distance, the other an edifice to a once familiar
touch, that was even then more a flowering abstinence,

but all of it honeycombed with secret passages between too
little and too much. Clouds now billow above skyscrapers
not like flowers but rather monstrous willows. All spawn of
a former life, smelling of summit stone, glacial silt and a lustrous

fragrance that makes gardens and rivers contract with shame:
cloud willows, though, just a bit too much? He's in a crowd,

if tenuously… one both inquisitive as insects, and annoying
as their bites; the more alone he feels the less he's let be:

how do things come to such a pass without ever passing
anything or letting it pass? He'll pass on that for the street
itself is changing fast as fashion while tenaciously holding
on to its name, clever as so many who are, indubitably, insane.

The wind works at flags with the same avidity as a crowd
using its abstract jaws and claws. No wonder he spends
his days painting colored arrows pointing to areas of the

unconscious still unexplored; undeveloped (how depressing
the number planted, how appalling the lack of grass,
let alone shrubbery, yet!) how long will the colors stay wet;

expressive? Or rather, will it be safe to go in when they dry?

And will it, no matter the case, lead to that particular "why"
that eludes here, or gain no more from it, when reached, than
the benefits of aftermath? But then all works ever made are

still waiting for the Second Coming of Inspiration to fill in
the gaps covered till now by the faith it does exist. As if in
response evening swells like a boil and as he walks he feels

it break, unseen, but releasing a lava-like anger; he would
swear he knows it, he should; it's from himself! Makes
twilight looks even thinner than his coat, shivering on the hills.

Stars then come out sharply, as if nailing down night as best
they can; and for no reason (it would be very disturbing if they

had one) they remind him of wall-flowers, how they were proms'
real themes – association piled on association though none of

them have even casually met… till he's finally distracted by
a pharmacy on the edge of town, an "INTIMATE ITEMS"
sale sign in blaring bordello red, soaked up by night like
evening's lava by an ever thirsty sea, a hiss, somewhere

between a swarm of bees and ebbing marine ecstasy slowly
drained by winter's obsidian regaining control of night. But
by the time that's resolved, or let hang as usual, he's already

back home at last, doesn't have to worry what else those
"somewheres" might hold only to find his painting appears
to have been attacked by claws and jaws – not the wind's
or the crowd's but the unconscious aroused and desperately,

directly, as if defending itself in the present rather than
through the customary channel of time-mangling dream,

which makes his waking so often unrecognizable as a conscious
state, leaving him like this painting, that is, as if he's been abused,

molested even though there is no evidence and despite that
he's still not sure, is never sure, if its due to his many
egregious mistakes or inspired as he felt about the painting
before and after... well it's still not after enough to decide

that yet! And if this be a flash of the brightness inside, why
then does he feel so darkly confused, and even shabbier than

the room? Night wrapping him tighter and tighter, like a
Christo of a greater world...will a metamorphosis have

occurred in him when he breaks free of this cocoon? For
all he's learned is, at it's best, to let tomorrow wrap tomorrow,
and poorly at that, as if it were a present not worth the effort;

and not even worth delivering it, and anyway there is no
address, can't be; and why not? For no other reason, he
learned from experience, than it's hard enough getting today
unwrapped from yesterday – and then being delivered of it.

If "Nearly" Were To Prove A Password…

I
Dawn sanding dark down; thinner; thinner; shadows for
a moment assume the shapes they've been denied,
or not allowed to retain, as theirs, for light, once through,

changing them and its other moods so fast, so fluidly,
even immediacy lags behind. He has no plan but

as things surface they accept what they find so why
should he get embroiled with "I am"? Shadow and
light then but two sides of time's endless, interior debate?
....
Perhaps profound, perhaps no more than reading oogamy
and thinking origami – still it seems each breaking

day is set to reconstruct perfection, not aware of course
that this light making it, is also what makes it fail at that.

Spotty moisture left by rain finds new purpose in
illuminating the cobwebs night wiled away its hours
with -- but why so large and intricate when all they
catch is small, often barely a flirt? One could ask

the same of mind-weave: how can truth slip through
untouched, but it does – shouldn't synapse density
alone snag it and even when making the slightest move?
....
The rapidly shifting, even swifter spread of these…
uncertainties – cannot distract him from the fact they
are surfaces, real surfaces, after all…"Nearly" he

thinks, that's as far as we get but --"it's no small

matter to be nearly living here"…"nearly" then more
like a password to further understanding than a mystery,
and close enough it shouldn't take forever to unlock,

yet far enough away, time alone won't get anyone
there; still, its tick the only evidence anything exists.

Horizons thus become palimpsests of surfaces built
up over the eons. They are nearer, nearly here, if one
considers where they started from…that is, from a

there looking so impenetrable he sometimes wonders
how we managed to get out in a single piece! (The
few clouds visible make the sky look amazingly
like the roughened palm of a worker's hand!)

II
Now it's light, he knows this cycle started long before
the night but just after the rain when it was… "nearly"

impossible to tell these two takes on dark apart. The
fading lightning set against, then amid, star spatter as it

emerged, having something of an exuberant Pollock flare
to it, but then he thinks of the size of the canvas and imagines
that expressionist working frantically, in growing despair!

But before the night and just after the rain the sky also
felt closer, almost a second skin, forming, being shed,
not close enough to tell, but in terms of self perhaps "I"
is all that's left of something rounder, with more heft.

And if "nearly" only works as a password between such
ticks, then that tight, miniscule distance may one day begin
to squeeze, to hurt... and...perhaps it would be better

to fear this "nearly", what it implies, or rather work to
remove the deadwood portions of our hearts, help them

recover their robust tree-like conviction that makes the
forest such an intimate but strange embrace for together,
thus, in a unique form of the singular, there is no exterior
or interior just an infinity of woven surfaces, so like the

sky, but now close as living skin. And the aloneness of it
itself is so immense and private even Plato's cave would

feel, would actually be, lost in it. A life of reflex and habit:
he started out forest-watching but became forest-preoccupied,

saw reflections of corridors and streets, the screams
imagined when silence exceeds even the most desperate
framing of a scene, creating the necessity of intersections

to distract him with notions of tracing out a labyrinth,
coupled with an inordinate fear of expresses always
running late, when any form of expression seems like

a reprimand, demanding an ever closer focus, an ever
more precise ambience, till one cannot tell going from
might have gone -- here gradually transformed into
there; no memory of transition to be found anywhere!

(Times like these he can almost imagine what the mind

will look like when so thought-scrambled it will take

a thought longer to cross it than it would the universe
though neither will be the same when the "crossing"
is crossed out!) Learn to watch the audience, he thinks,

the way it takes in a play, a film, watch, he thinks, as
if he were the director, only on a larger set: how far then
can intimacy be spread and still matter as much in that

moment to just him, just you, just us? Nearly as far as
the sensation when the call comes for "action"; not
nearly far enough to counteract the loss of touch at "cut"?

"Nearly" could be a password for like passwords it doesn't
link – only gets one in, is of no help in getting one out again.

On Butterflies, Mandlebrot And Silver Lining Departments

Light bursts night's sack of dew and dawn's wind
atomizer spreads it as mist. A whole age could be
passing through, soaking slowly; unknowingly –

as if preparing itself for how dry it's about to get?
Much the same as when a child discovers grass is
deeper in more ways than it could have imagined
just yesterday but now knows as well how to prepare
his fantasies before tomorrow can make its case!
....
Shadows of departing buccaneers still cling to the
school flagpole/mast, though land has been espied.
Morning wakes like a lion, long on limb stretch

and yawn, testing the full extent of the dominion
imposed by the mere weight of its muscular repose.
....
If this were as private as it feels, his intrusion would
certainly… stimulate a most unwelcome appetite.

The wind's warmth would then almost fatefully acquire
the feel of rippled fur, insect scraping of claw and so
on – how aroused the hum of engine driving its breath!

Piracy? Lions? Why do such anachronisms still persist
in these post-inhabitable, ballistically global, days?
....
Let rant then find its own tenor; let time slip, as it slips
by; let doubt spring a leak, run out: for weather is on
a course no one would have predicted and who wants

to be blamed for making a prediction now? For a while
it seemed butterflies and Mandelbrot had been ruined

but since then he's learned the rudiments of fractal-
shuffle and signing in butterfly; and in tandem learned

they're both wrong a lot. Justice, he thinks, to sound
positive, and where it's least expected... and he already
regrets having revealed that. But the brook pays no

notice, as it tumbles down the ruffled rocks. And his
mind remains ruffled as well, but with a turbulence that
could no longer stand the lackadaisical rhythms of
the sea playing the role of eternity, and thinking that

by now it must be the play -- keeps turning the volume
up, as if it were thinking deep and hard, ruffling its

surface, then smoothing it suddenly, as if showing its
concentration is that intense, or perhaps signaling some-
thing it didn't want him to learn about... directly... but

knew he must know, making the silence reappear like a
diver but one he'd been sure had been lost, and the meaning

of it bursts upon him – you must go down to understand up,
must go up to understand down, and all that intervenes
is a world of bubbles like from the diver's suit while the
air itself is colored and effervescing like the finest champagne

whose cork had just been popped. And he unconsciously
and automatically pops his ears, the sense of it all was

so strong, so clear and knowing then that if one's friends

claim to be experts at any part of this, consider fear as
their only other possible option. Odd isn't it how belief
is a fear of the unknown while knowing welcomes it!
....
The sun immediately turns up the heat, as if it's about
to take an epic step. And by afternoon, sure enough,
mythic shapes begin to appear under cover of pea-size-

fetus clouds. What do heroes say when they're called
into such a breach? What would you say if you were

brought up on immortality? "Let's get going it'll be a
madhouse at the beach." "Where the fuck did you put
those keys this time?" "You didn't what?" "You did what?"

Some times the world is so transparent he's surprised
things have managed to find anything to hold on to at all!
....
The outré charade of shadows, however, would not, by
that alone, he's sure, be forestalled. For he remembers
when she said, "truth is a slippery, skittery thing; likes to
talk of futures with averted eyes". Usually she remained

hidden in her unpolished silver mood-hood at times like
those, so he never learned if the words or attitudes came
first, or if their order symbolized a excess, or lack, of choice.

She also spoke of wing rhythms, and they were clearly a clue, but
her tone made it even clearer he would get into their beat –

her eyes were averted when she said it and he's slow on

picking up clues and anyway he got the gist and the future
where only truth could possibly exist became a two-sided

cliff; her side had rope, his string; now who could tell which
would prove more... instrumental in the end...he noted,

laughed as she did – and she it turned out had the last one –
that is, he could have it too, but who wants to laugh alone.

So, for now he'll index it under butterflies and Mandelbrot
while night's sack is hung out to drain and dry.
He'll know it's empty when it suddenly turns blue.
....
The mist disappears in one last gust like a swarm of
bees off to found a hive; in number about the same
as the times he started trying to say goodbye but

memory as always, makes him lose heart while hope
parts such emotional Red Seas easily, though it tends
to forget where it is when it's half way across!

There is, always, however, the honey of the moment
to collect if one isn't allergic to the stings, and if he

really did let bygones be bygones then he'd have
nothing to look forward to, but also nothing to regret.

For while the landscape on its own tends toward capriccio
as mist, bees letting bygones be keep it firmly terrace-laced.
So, live here long enough, he thinks, and you know

one day it will stop you as you pass and tell you how
things stand, face to face. Time then will laugh insanely

and reason, not understanding, will look askance as
thought splits its sides with delight! Meaning: he's glad

she came to him before she left. Because she made it
clear from the start she wouldn't put up with too much
of that. But let's not be so quick with names this time,

he suggests if only to himself; be sure they fit. Come
over here, where the shade's more capacious, though

he's also aware it's far too late to begin or even end, like
this, so he addresses the shadows, she's almost one of

them now (time, oh the time!) and can being here compensate
for the futility of exposing either of them, living and
not to the consequences of "we should be getting back"?

So Where Is The Who, And Who Cares?

The palisades shaving off their ice with a sun blade,
steaming morning's mirror.

His mirror notes both, refuses to admit their resemblance
but then it has always kept the best
stuff to itself – is that why it
finds it hard to look him straight in the eyes?

The air, more secure with itself, willing to share its
elegy to clarity, delivered in light
hitting dew, the tiniest of pings! Or here
on the beach, a coin that just fell
on coarse sand. How many drafts of that will

he have made before he can decide…which is more
fitting and most likely to abide? What
influence will death have had on its thematic drift?

A nearly imperceptible melding of equally
imperceptible impingements on sense –
or a sudden, catastrophic, and also imperceptible shift?

(Dreams may hold the answer but even computers haven't
broken their code – seems there are things
we have to know but not, at any cost, understand.)

So for now it's just air! branches unmoving, emitting
the kitten-like mews of baby birds or
the sorrow of a timid owl, or the smothered
moan of something deep in a rut

running out of refuse-to-give-up excuses,

knowing it's now on its own, but by the time these sensations
reach him they too have been transformed, have become
a subtle and undefined essence of a turbulent
mind blindly feeling the contours of
the inside of his face -- as if seeking where
similar feelings have gone to hide.

Naming the echoes of each silence could be the name of this
game. The original only mirrors know how to
trace – and completing the imperfect circle: seldom with grace.

....

While the light moves the day quite effortlessly through
the huge obstruction called nature though
by late afternoon the shadows do
show some distraction, shapes distended and well…
shapeless trying to get out while staying, somehow, in the way.

The luminance being lowered they no longer need to
offer any sense of relief. And who
would have thought morning so freshly
rubbed clean would become in just a few hours

a receptacle for mushrooms steaming on a rotting log,
drawing on a store of unsuspected and
repulsive heat or that by evening a
hot rain would fall, pungent as vulture piss?
(He's seen vultures idly sky-doodling,
smelled their virulent piss – it's a no-brainer.)

....

And now as light loses its cathartic ability to inspire
the senses, lightning sets free its serpents

which seem almost obscenely eager to draw
scurrilous designs on its carcass,
infusing evening's still gestating vermilion made

disgusting with a dab of a sickly toad-gloat hue: things
seem to have suddenly sprung leaks,
each with its own drip, appear
vulnerable to the threat from above, like
having a "this is your life moment" and only being
shown the last few seconds – it's absurd

but he curses himself anyway -- why didn't I sell while I
had a chance he thinks, I should have known
the upkeep would cost more than the
land, the house, would ever be worth and how much
land does a man require, Tolstoy was no fool –

knew there are always more and more "somethings" to
attend to and it gets harder and
harder to set priorities, to resolve them into
what was once anyway the simplest form of choose.

For we're not swallows (he thinks as one works yet another
routine, so tireless, so inventive at making the
same way look new every time, using
the nest as an excuse he thinks,
taking a chance the storm or night will fall before…
who cares!) though we swerve as much, more
clumsily, and often too late and…
and may well show a barely supressed aversion to nests.
....
Now evening's fully collapsed it's almost like the
morning except for the dark's unspoken

but voice-filled weight, clearly wanting to
tell him of all he missed, eager to inform him
there's a crush up ahead and no one
knows or has ever learned later what it's a crush of?

Yet everyone seems certain it's symbolic of a future state –
will we forever be debating if its inside or
outside the strict but secretly timed limits…no, contours,
of our fate? Night knows but it ain't talkin'…
not yet… come in door's always open…didn't I say, not yet!
　　　　………………………………………
For… he still doesn't have a porch or a breakfast to
eat on it. That ought to do as an excuse
till he can come up with a reason, or better,
a better excuse and… and night-vision goggles
still remain, just after day-vision spectacles
that would reveal well… the full spectacle of what

must lie right before his eyes in plain sight – is that the
problem – its plain while sight itself is so
complicated? no wonder they both come far
before thinking good thoughts -- on his Later List.

Meanwhile, the roof keeps shunning his attempts at repair,
infuriating really as it acts if it had just
learned from forever the secret of wait and why,
tell me why, he says to himself, we have to
face each other like…flagellants over a Lenten meal
and just because he said he'd walk across live coals for

her, you that is, it's easy to confuse the living with the dead –
couldn't she, you, understand the irony
of him saying all this as if it were true, while standing

there, of all paces, at the grille!

(Why does he feel alone when experience itself proves
he's not? And why does it so often feel,
when he's thinking, that he's talking to himself –
when that part of him is never there, then?)

Reduced now to making doodles and half-assed
metaphors on a pad (to think it was
thought of as an achievement once!) still trying to
re-trace the course of a face emerging from
a mirror more devious than any maze, afraid, it

would seem, of reawakening immaculate desire, having
decided it was time to give toxic a chance
to be put to better use... he knows, and
knows he knows; so where is the who, and who cares?
ANOTHER TOMORROW HE COULDN'T JUST WAIT
AROUND FOR

The mind plays with the aspects of could be, could be
not, soothed by the ebb and flow of
vitality, monotonously, almost hypnotically
like a litany in a dead tongue.

Feeling itself to be filling slowly, oh so deliciously slowly
with all the possibilities offered by a
field covered in dew, but where in a sudden
and urgent blazing of light it realizes only partial
directions are encoded in a day's genome.

Later the dust comes seeping as if it had heard it too, but
cannot understand; for here where mighty

sounds are all muffled, indistinguishable as static,
hearing even a small but clear tinkle can make
not only him but even the world seem inordinately proud!

And though part of (what isn't), does not. like the EXIT
sign on the rink that had a short and flashed
senselessly, making him so uncomfortable –
as if he were watching someone having a stroke.

Summer passed but the rink remained bald despite troupes
of experts submitting plans for a turf toupee.
The sign fixed -- but the exit moved elsewhere.
There were many other parts but after that he didn't
even bother looking for an entrance, exits be damned!
....
So, afternoon already, fog rolling in like distance collapsing,
parameters shifting as inevitably as the stations
leading to the climactic moment of
the Passion, now referred to, to avoid confusion,
as Sex, so resurrection is ironic if not anticlimactic, at best.

Anyway, echoes encapsulated in nearly invisible bubbles
of mist carried here from who knows where:
bamboo flutes, sirens, mice-phobic screams erasing
decibels as fast as they're made, or
unfathomable...emissions; commissions he'd like to say

of an unapproved act but that's not a decision he would,
even if he could, make – anyway, not the usual...
claustrophobic sense of an unwanted intimacy,
but rather an opaque Doppler pulsation of what's coming,
but only reaches him when it's already far away.
A wanted intimacy that is but one nonetheless, refused.

(Though it too depends on memory and thus brings up
the inherent contradiction of lingering in said
memory, especially when one knows
what vital details are being continually, irrevocably, lost --

think of the silence unique to the inside of a bell – though it
could just be metal gone deaf he supposes –
or, better, the senses protecting their private anagrams
for his (and anyone's, anyone like him at least)
fading name – seems the only way to
insure the effect on the butterfly of the Butterfly Effect.)

And though the wine may now be vinegar the stains still
retain a...certain jubilance from when the
tumblers were first filled with it, the rejoicing throats....
enough to toast his childhood with now, late
of course but in the circumstances certainly allowed:
like being inside a poem and thinking one's speaking out loud.

And like that (how can it feel so close to this? and after all
this time!) the evening is over, but the night yet
to begin. Reflections from an unseen sea outline the
stones on a hill so they appear to be a fallen family tree
of a mad race determined to somehow survive, form irrelevant –

better fog, but viewed as clay's next potentiality. All to be
treated as signs of another tomorrow he can't just wait
around for while each breath takes away what once was
considered to be a vital part of him – each time moving
it just that much further from where he's trying to breathe.

Time, Time, Time…

In his full, secondhand, winter regalia he might be taken
for a cult figure in an Eskimo Museum.
If there was one, if he felt like kidding himself that he
needed a non-existent museum to take his
mind off this ridiculous weather where just going
out makes him look the perfect fool, imperfecting himself.

He knows how he got here, but memory is self-serving,
turns impulsive decisions into no other way
it could have been done; and why does anyone
live here, why do we extol these extremes of nature
at the antipodes, not as malign, perhaps,
as urban decay -- but with much the same result?

Is it so crucial to his sense of self esteem that patches of ice
on roofs seem like icons hung on dead-stars realm of fate?

Not that he's forgotten, he just can't remember…specifically,
what he used to casually recall without giving
it a thought.(Specifics were rare back
then -- the general alone could get pretty hot!)

But then age is always plagued by so much nagging "ought".
And he does feel closer to the cold rain,
especially when it devotes days in
convincing the ground it deserves no better than
mud, before freezing it quickly, painting it white and refusing

to admit there ever was such a thing as "bare ground",
especially when claimed as a "ground for

belief". More or less how he tries to feel about
himself, at least when someone might be
looking, laughing, when there's nothing to laugh at,
that he can see, and even when looking back.

The sky now wearing a grim winter frown. A reminder of
the look of the ground when it was bare but
friable; not frozen yet, only lightly ice-basted... just a taste.

Some asshole wearing sunglasses just walked into a wall.
He thinks, as if shaken by hitting some inner
wall of his own, of all his reflections he missed
and now never to be seen, and if Mr. Sunglasses
Asshole will live to regret that...

the rest of that thought will fit better in another poem, later,
later anyway as he's likely to get...and whatever
the case he's already been distracted and quite
unconscionably, if he may say so by the sheer amount of frozen

phlegm outside this... what else, bar, bugs and dead dragons
from a lost Age, that if it were found would be
re-lost much better this time and... as can
be observed, he observed...this could still be...
anywhere, though here, at least, it would be more
like nowhere at all, that is, till he discovers
he's looking in a mirror on the inside of the bar
except he's warm ordering an expensive drink... just isn't fair!

To hide his chagrin, being reminded of the life he might have
led with money and being able in that other life to
hold his drink and not just in his hand... he
quickly enters a theme mall, or so he guesses, as it's like

entering an old mine shaft supported on rickety metal (plastic?)
columns with veins of Day-Glo gold, large enough
to overload a mother of a mother lode.
A woman is buying a miner's hat and a lamp and...
putting her sunglasses back on!

More reflections to reflect upon but they're as smudged
as the theme inside the mall. No one would
believe any of this if seen in stills. Still,
what's a mine without a still and sure enough
there it is – at the head of the shaft!

Time, time, time. Time a palimpsest, time a frozen mist,
time an arrow, time a spider trying to
undo the havoc the head has played with its
web, time failing to untangle it, time
moving into deep space so at least its cries won't
be heard, time erasing the present because
there is never enough to go round... at any one time,

time the artifact, the fact, the art, time that leaves one
in the middle of something just the same way
it supplies dots to fill the gaps in his
metaphysics and if there's time to step back
into physical reality, strengthened by them, he may
yet come to understand why God gave up on

this line of thought... and finding that line of thought about
as physical as a wet rag, if he thinks of something
else in time he'll give it a shot, a kick, a kiss,
that is, if he hasn't by then entered the time zone of better not.

But retrospect, he's found, is like that little Italian place that
made its own pasta and wine but for some silly reason
no one can remember was converted into
a secondhand store, catering to the Lesser of the
Great Unwashed. Not that he's complaining –
it's only natural that the free coffee and stale
muffins taste like reactor meltdown mixed with mold, and

speaking of things radioactive, the place also has a view of
the two-sided church on the only hill around,
one that was never completed once it
was revealed the hill had been a toxic waste site
once, and that once, in half-life lingo, is
almost geological in scope – and yet the building went on

(fanatics revel in toxic stuff, being as near to their dream
home, to the full-life, as they will ever achieve
on Earth) but after (reputedly, fireworks suspected) a few,
small leaks, dramatic as geysers, but too close to

Rapture-rapture as they conceived it at least, just never,
but never coming out of the ground – it suddenly
felt hot as Hell in short…and anyway, it now
seems when the facts and their apparently final fictional
twists, are in – and have had time to be palatably

swallowed in a sugar-and-spiced suspension of disbelief mode,
the "they", the builders that is, have by now been
whittled to one, some lunatic (one the others
worshipped, by the way, like a saint or would have if they

had believed in saints, but since they didn't, one of the
light-seers then, from I-could-see-and-now-

I'm-blind side of the street, that is, so central to
their hagiography though icons themselves were anathema –

something snakes might bite when they couldn't get
through the God-field surrounding those of faith...)
anyway! "they" the future worshippers, that is,
though they did it somewhere else, wing
and a prayer location most probably, and the lunatic who
took the occasional nocturnal spectral sparkle

seen there as a sign from Above and so went to work, with
nothing but snakes wrapped round him, like
phylacteries oddly enough, a trowel, stones, cement,
faith he supposes... in a dark that glowed (still
does though there's little of the Lord's dark around anymore)

anyway! the brochure on "The Church of the Half-Life
Rapture" states unequivocally that he died while
digging the last part of the foundation, bitten
by a "fallen" viper and his "tongues" then swelled
to such an enormous size, his faith had no way to express

itself and so he choked on his own true belief – "madder than
Jesse's adder" now part of the local patois; some
say it's pathetic, others that it's pretty neat, while still
others – there aren't any or at least they don't give a vocal shit.

A storm is building, (odd phrase really since storms tear down)
and the few people inside, all strategically placed, so
the abstract gleam drifting about in their eyes
will have places to focus that aren't unfathomably
far away or so close they might be dangerous,

like a sudden intersection of many rails might be. It's all they
have to compete for – in this phantom light
anyway whose "half" life isn't the half of it. He, on the other

hand, thinks of salamanders and jasmine, of John Cage at
a Sessions session, elephant graveyards and
how long before the ground starts to shake when
the extinct but not forgotten volcano starts
to growl; or why La Monte Young is still viewed

by many as an avatar of the future of our DNA: in short
what is the origin and true nature of "expect"?

By now the coffee's fuel rods seem to be spent, and the muffins
are reconsidering their crumbs, while a derelict on
his way to the homeless shelter is blown by
like a chunk of befouled snow the plough just pushed
up on the curb, and all of them, even those in the midst of their

abstraction, heave a sigh. There but for… and work on a private
lie that someday they still hope to patent, maybe even
win a prize for it. He walks out into the snow,
each step counter-punching the wind, wishing his
home was a Museum, not just a place to store
memorabilia he's not even sure are his… and not all

that memorable… which brings him back to the Eskimo
Museum and time, time, time, and the fact that
none of it is anything he could ever even…
pretend was his; nor what he might even find in its
ever growing and complexifying web, as it
maddeningly passes him by, while even more maddeningly

staying right here! inside! but in a place he can't reach! Called
uncertainty but with far more certainty than any
belief: so sure of itself it's never quizzed
him even once on where he came up with
the idea of, found the time, (made it, goddamn it!),
to dream up his apparently unobserved, self.
But dreams are not the stuff time's made of, nor is the self.

Temporarily Untitled
(Till He Finds The Fit For His Life Therein)

Day opens. Phlegm-thick fog hawked from the throat
of night; some unfinished business probably; not

anyway a case of all or nothing; it's just the boundaries
between them cannot be recalled. The fog thins, or swells,

with light, at least acts less ghoulish, less like ghost
decay, closer to the helplessly and ever so softly,

flailing limbs of an infant enjoying this self it's growing
into, having no idea it's on the verge of learning what it

means to be alone, open to the experience of being undone,
made helpless all over again by what he'll learn from it.

When it finally clears the day is already in the midst of
inspiring and expiring, so there is no greater or lesser view;

a twist of trees shaking the wind out of their leaves, a
weaving of their reflections disclosing a slather of sexual

oil applied, and in a way he dreamed would be used on
his sleeping form, ivy curling round the window as if

waiting to have a peek, never knowing it's the beauty he
so longs to be inside of, to be peeking thus; that such

symmetry of purpose, such elegant misdirection, is able to
choreograph this life; then doing much the same with death.

Keep life close like a friend, or closer, like an enemy? What
is he to think of those who think this makes perfect sense?

Why not loosen things up, see what he can make of the folds
unfolded? If the heat responds, as it might, move on to wonder,

quickly, hoping to catch it napping, get it thus to reveal its shape.
While carrying on, trying to make something of wind-whoosh,

siren-binge, frantic fly-fringes obstructing the eyes, rain
working at his features obsessively as if they were stone,

with no design inside, finding flesh is the hardest material
known, -- and despite all that also finding the eye keeps

drifting back to an endlessness of sky. A cry required?
Triumph? Despair? Without more to go on: must

language then fall back on idealization, the oh so devious,
oh so alluringly wicked twin of sight? Or rather a way to

"accomplish a longer existential leap into metaphysical
eminence, wanting to excel at momentum, at the transformation

of loss..." a thought he noted as he turned to the mail, letting
the words of ads, bills, letters, trigger thoughts like the changing

rhythm of drips falling from eaves after rain, imagining the rain,
finding unsuspected harmonies in soil, which feels impelled,

it would seem, to help the roots reach what they're rooting for;
all our lives enriched by these things beyond our ken, or theirs:

so the world can remain a constant reminder of being taken
by surprise? Why does it seem quite natural that his reading

and the dripping should both stop at the same time? Is it
because we learn the world only works by accident upon accident,

no one ever knowing what to expect; and so far it seems to have
come prepared for anything – everything, the vote's still out.

As now, reaching the stage of summer where each living
thing achieves some private definition of green, and even

the mountains are tinged a whimsical elfin hue, while down
here it's fragrances and experimenting with wind, making for

a vast room full of aromatic and tinted air developing that
most delicious sense of the ever… vulnerable: that so much

of where he happens to be is, and will remain, precisely
what he can't find a way to fathom though having the

advantage of time making it discrete, but despite that the flow
is so relentless it's past before they can meet. No net "catches

change on the wing" as Monod surmised evolution did. Not
this change anyway which, paradoxically, is always the same.

A car races by hitting every bump on the dirt road as if on a
bombing raid: jays and crows squabble in the dust, staking

claims on the varying silences filling the gaps in the car's
chaotic wake, so adroitly he's certain their choices are not by

mistake, though to him the bumps seemed totally alike... and
all the while, unaffected, cancers grow, tea steeps, cinnamon

gets spicier, mold spreads, candles flare and fade pulling after
them their light – and as if he alone were in possession of

this marvelous form of sight! So experience in itself does
mean something, even when it doesn't go the way he expects

and getting deeper than that requires another experience, so
he will never learn if days are loops of a certain size we're all

orbiting till gravity collapses them upon us, or more like strings
and complex manifolds but only going far enough to hint

we're on a bifurcating trail that will in some landscape
eventually lead to the den of the Minotaur, but never in any

landscape indicating which part leads into, which out of.
Metaphysically it makes little difference: the labyrinth

is always longer than any thread. The Minotaur not nearly
as ferocious as the dead-end it has to contain its fury in.

So: "temporarily untitled" till he finds the fit for his life therein.

An Embrace

Sudden unmistakable feel of an old, familiar embrace –
but so old there's no trace of either of them inside.

He looks around: nature seems even smaller than in
memory, with fewer places to hide in, or where he'd

want to hide, anyway. Autumn rain: the color and
consistency of mother's milk. Yards of chaotically

scattered leaves, hills of fright-wig vineyards, grave-
yards lining up their memorials at the edge of town:

in the hope death evolves a need for society? Clouds
sit like misshapen loaves in a bin: an image of the edible,

begging to be let in. A pliable swarm of insects doing
sketch after sketch of a face and he realizes how a

name can also be a private anonymity. Two halves of a
meaning he'd thought would be easy to join together

till he learned there was no true fit; even dead we do
poorly, once underground anyway. Absence and presence;

thoughts hung out to dry unseen except for the breeze
they displace. The insects now absorbed in all forms

of bark while he imagines twisting trails as wagging tails
on the unicornish body of Utopia! So when the moon

rises tonight he will try to rise with it. If there were only a
celestial photographer to catch them in a passionate embrace!

Thoughts that clearly derive from living close to the sea
where even they have to shout to be heard in his mind

that is and thus tend to become exaggerated and loose in
the same way he is inclined to talk about these thoughts —

when not thinking them, at least. Of course he only lives
near cliffs that were once near the sea as their fossils indicate

and which now are crumbling so fast they seem to know
it's time to come to terms with the return of that sea.

Then again it could just be a natural romanticism turning
the hardening carapace of the living into a ceremony

where everything is simply washed away, casually. Did
the embrace remind him of this or this the embrace?

Both bring to mind the fact the Earth is an assemblage
of all the hints the sky has dropped or taken to their

extreme – and regardless of what miracles goddesses
may have planned: the sky's grip on reality no better than

the one consciousness has, and needs Earth's comprehensive
protean inclusion, its embrace, as well -- if it hopes to survive.

Starting With A Leaf And A River

A leaf swirls round on a river and the poem is given
cause to wonder if this is not symbolic of the way
things are within itself -- so casually mocked by much

deeper things? Were the fish biting or not; what kind,
and were they biting each other too? How much
depends on what each of us does, on what we all do?

If it were dead cigarettes and silhouettes would it be
much the same? Even if all ass-wipes were let loose at once?

Etc. filling the margins beside the opening lines while
inspiration runs make-believe but urgent errands for
wannabe people – and they are in more immediate need.
....
Shadows going by the window, like scenes plagiarized
from the Ministry of Funny Walks, but looking out he
saw only the familiar tedious patterns of hopheads and
amnesiacs on their way to work, unaware, or it would

seem, "jobs" no longer exist, discounting sleep, but then
a neighbor kept shaking her finger at her mynah bird

though she must know by now it will never learn to
say more than "it's a crock". "Crests, tufts, plumes"
he whispers to the pleated room when, without any

seismic warning, windows along the street begin to
ripple and for some reason he thinks of an immense
but invisible cascading harp that can't seem to stop itself;

sounds a maniac might hear when running water begins
to weave his hands into bouquets that move to his face

and set about slowly smothering him. He takes this
as a plea to heed the caution implied by the preceding
lines: the poem may make it all up but that does not
preclude a profounder, and far more disturbing, source.

Making faces while twirling a hat on its linguistic thumb,
acting like an idiot till one simply knows it can't be that dumb.

The world, however, is aware of none of this, of how
things manage to become more than they are, and on their

own, all these mynahs and nightingales, disgusting pigeons
and irascible geese, the wind tunnel that suddenly appeared,
stripped people naked, mixed the numbers on prices in
stores and even swept the last frail maiden from the town's

only remaining bridge -- both innocent of suicide! And
what about the origami class that specialized in "creative"

Calabi-Yau manifolds, or the anonymous donor of those
7 exquisitely framed and embroidered representations of

the Deadly Sins to the local museum and why it took it so
long to discover that the "embroidery" was actually made

of pulverized children's bones? On the other hand, it takes
considerably longer to accept the end is always, stunningly,
abrupt, like the sound of a ledge crumbling after one falls
from it, or, perhaps, it's in the looking down, the rapid

narrowing of distance, while thinking "water is always open"
and wondering, if ever so briefly – how something so solid,
still flows; and why is it so hard to learn with all we know?

While it's not hard to imagine, once he accepts anyway that
a moment has more time in it than he'll ever have time to use.

Why then shouldn't he fill it with the sweet dark nothings
of soaring choruses, promising; promising...buttressed by

nothing but what was always the elegance inherent in air
lending itself so graciously to flight, and with the same

elegance of a woman lifting a glass, knowing, without
looking, that the wine is already being poured. That even
the roughest surface will eventually be recycled, refined,

in this way, and even the most subtle, sublime and deepest
needs of a person will rise to that ever shuffling surface

to be refurbished, made simpler and yet more exquisite:
leaf, river, poem, even himself. Then perhaps the one and
the many will at last be seen as an endlessly specialized
collection of reflections of things, only visible till now to

the 6th or higher senses, it appears, though even they are
hard-pressed to imagine this ever ongoing something
is ever and always and instantly...something else...

that this form of recycling demands, that every thing
needs as well to be... well, everything, with water, always,
somewhere, winding/unwinding; the elusive, ever-present,

go-between. The poem, too, must become such a surface
so when he holds it up to the window the leaves hidden

in it will suddenly come out and just as they would if on
a tree itself, which come out like the stars which…

and for that… moment it's not hard to understand why he
encourages his self to see itself as acting exactly like that.

On Interpretation Of Patterns And Being...Circumspect

The room went full yellow, not even the sky was able to
handle the afterglow; the wind rose to panic state, blindly
flailing around, losing its way, always finding another nearly

as good again, "nearly" in the sense of those who are sure
they know a quicker route and yet always come in lagging
far behind. And he kept thinking of the mind coming at

thought from all directions with arguments for immortality ...
then: perish the thought! But when thoughts become even

more outrageous than that, and they do, if things get that drastic,
it's time to call the re-router in, and he never is, in, that is.
....
It should have been getting darker and the unnatural yellow
faded as if pretending it was doing just that. But everything
was still too bright for the amount of purple compressing

the western sky. Not counting the light from other sources
that should have run out of time. Something he never
suspected but already so far advanced in happening, he should
have – after all did it have any other choice but to appear?

Why then does it seem most dangerous when it should, on the
surface anyway, have nothing to do with him – could it be
because his actions, even these lines, show just the opposite?
....
He watched a spider weave a greeting card flower-web in a
corner of the room, thought for some reason of a Babylonian

maxim he'd seen inscribed on a fresh grave, and wondered
if it was serious or not. It said: "now the vanity of existence
looks in vain for an excuse." Anyway, that's what someone,

and a joker at that, said it said but it's still all Babylonian to
him, might be telling him no more than "so the ditch gets fed."

The wind may still have been blind but it had also regained
its blurring "touch", infusing the world with a subtle shimmer
and as carefully as Monet and all the while not a single word
except in his head -- fish in a school but probably learning less?

Like most things: momentum must be gained, but what leads
to the momentous will never thus be explained; for now it
was night working on its map of the psyche after an interlude

of evenings of rain though it still wasn't clear if the light or
dark areas were more significant -- and to whom and for what
reason. The breeze did have a more confident whisper as it

ran its fingers over the wheat stubble as if it were a beard
before a shave. If he'd been a painter he would have forgotten

to eat or have painted it long before night fell, or maybe have
had no interest at all but having nothing better to do then…

he did have vodka and cheese, labels in Chinese (who
knows why as he was told both said "Product of France").

To him it looked more like several alphabets cut up by a
lunatic and stuck together with that peculiar logic a madman
has so impatiently developed, so eerily universal it's hard to
believe it's mad. When he mentioned it someone not listening

said it's not dangerous, at least not in that way and some of the
alphabet splinters can even mean quite esoteric things. People!
....

Oddly enough when twilight fell so did he, spraining his
knee as a consequence. Glad he'd reached the end of
the street by then and was halfway back, -- and still watching

yellow seep into dark. Using his new found limp with pizzazz
or so he imagined it, like someone pissing while practicing
ballet steps – anyway, he soon devised a unique syncopation

for his walk, employing the faltering light for the basic
rhythm, leaning toward a far-off veil of rain to get its
swoop into his gait, as well as an unseasonable shivering

as if to hurry the limp along, leaving pauses and lapses in
unexpected places so if anyone was watching they would

think he was looking for something and…or at least not
notice the limp though it was actually by then far more
distinguished that his usual shuffling along. Maybe someone

did look up then from reading the instructions on his new
medication or video game and briefly believed he was finally

making something out of himself. He felt almost hurried, or

rather harried by the scream of the evening express and gave
yellow no more thought till now as things have loosened their

daily forms and gone back to being mediums, crying out for
a wordsmith's ingenuity, rising randomly into the velvet

evening like quantum yeast, bread perhaps he would break
come some tomorrow, assuming the yellow context remained

evidence of a transformation that though far too advanced to
be undone and still too early in his discovery program to know

what it might do next, he could nonetheless be confident that
given time he could make sure it never got... completely done.

Thus he returned to the splendid understanding of his chair
which helped him understand how one might view "I" as a
composite of variable patterns of "we" but the instantaneous

change inflicted upon him by each fresh moment means the
interpretation of the patterns must be done very, very... circumspectly.

On How Things Are Stacked

Sunny today, spring they say, but if so it's spring
straight from the witch's tit; (even her witch-lings
won't give suck and indeed give the old hag the
"broom"). And the subway never stops grumbling

as it follows him from bar to bar where witches are
thawing out their swollen, icy dugs and talking
about being bewitched -- like others do about their

"bewitching" youth. The rumbles run deeper and are
too widespread to be just from trains; more like
composites of how it feels to be stranded in life by

accident, without the force or the will to set oneself
free. He had had what it takes but someone, some thing

must have taken it from him or more likely he left it
somewhere in those vast distances the mind thinks
it is obliged to visit as the self-appointed and
official representative of the center of the universe.

It's not only he doesn't believe, he doesn't want to, or
even be associated with those who do, belief doing
nothing but throwing knowing off the scent of truth.

Meaning he has to invent endings all on his own,
arriving at himself and in the same way history does
at now "just knowing this was the place, somehow",

that this was the way, anyway, things would have to

turn out. Not quite self-delusion, history really does

get here that way, more like assembling a kit where
some of the key parts are missing and one then has
to improvise, which brings him back to history as

subjectivity objectified, as if reaching here involved
an almost cabalistic process of successive stages of
sleepwalking – and wondering how far yet to wake.

In any case, he never thought, "I can be anything I
want to be"; it was hard enough to act like himself
and not like someone he met who looked at him long

and quizzically. That "anything" is the never-mentioned
mystery so willing to be there and help one find a
way out from where there is said to be no escape,
making sure one's ignorance of this stays topped

up and the odds are so stacked against one he'll
give "anything" the benefit of the doubt; the Nazis

used those "benefits" that way and they're still not
used up. Hire an illegal, slip him a counterfeit bill,
when he's deported feel good like a patriot should.

And things are stacked against us all, and variously;
those swollen traffic jams that will eventually like a

tsunami inundate the city, say, or maybe nothing more
than some scattered bones, filthy snow-banks, perverted
moms: don't even bother to run the prints or have the
DNA analyzed. Most have been given ancestral immunity

or were donated in the form of "pledged" donations to
charities that fund those very stacks so uncharitably, like

a bank giving huge bonuses to its most incompetent
employees; all of it, in any case, set against him,
repeatedly. Where does he think the green came from

for that monstrosity called the Memorial to the Dead of
Future Wars that seems to wrap around him like a

living labyrinth while at the same time refusing to
take him inside, leaving him, as it were, at the center

of a writhing universe that longs to, (but physics is
determined to prevent it from doing so), collapse…

for though the mind may be a work in progress it
seems to have hit a snag, run out of grants or got
conned into trying to develop something special for

each of the 10^{500} landscapes so dimensionally strung-
out it's hard to tell if they're even there, so he's not

amazed when he begins to calculate what that much
string would…cost – assuming that it could be
found, because the dimensions can't. So he drinks,

chain-smokes, wonders how days come to be only
noticed when they become X-rays of night; afraid

to love, afraid someone else might catch what's
infecting him or be the source of something else

far worse itself: a concentration camp, say, where

he'd be unable to concentrate; if God made us in his
image He should have taken a longer, closer look before... .

Cold Probability Or Warm Mystery?

Or perhaps something that has to be but hasn't been
as yet -- though the day be large with almost fleshy
clouds, slightly feminine, more than slightly erotic...

the distance between them still leaves features, even
whole faces, to the imagination -- a dokini, a female
Buddha, in what will pass for ultimate flesh, at last?

Or just the concept of shave taken to a higher level,
to where the complete removal of identity is complete?

All that, but there is also the steam filling out the matrix
of his mirror, seductive shapes of spiritual semen
released, preening for some reason – is this the way
they would like to see themselves looking in a dream?

If he were reborn would he have the sexy predator's
eyes he's always dreamed of but with a stranger's

transcendent mentality, unshakable morality? Imagine
the challenge of keeping such contradictory hungers aligned!

Shadows, waves, cliffs, even whole mountains shaking
loose their tectonic threads like vermin being combed
from a beard. Rivers appearing out of nowhere, stones

seemingly drought-immune now standing even more
erectly in a flood; the sky has evidently blinded its own

eyes and sent fingers of light fumbling rain to excavate

the pummeled banks. Awakening he rushes to the
window to make sure it's keeping up with developments;
just barely and not really viably, in any case.

So many poses, so little time to consider why there's
a need; what is it he must see while not suspecting

what it'll prove to be? Entering each like a gallery when
no one's there; studded boots, fuck-me pumps, belts,
straps, halters, fur-braided whips, goose-pimple dildos,

thinking: how did he come to look for the intimate here,
what made him think it had something guilty to hide?
....
Two deer move along the edge of the woods, a mobile
tapestry; hills colliding with clouds so they can collapse

and become a part of what creation is getting round to,
but… not…yet? Butterflies, wasps, gnats, weave through
and in time each of their spaces will become a vital

though unseen knot. If he were a swallow…then there,
and while the knot was still flexible, he would build his
nest! The mind clambers eagerly in realms missed out on
by the real and thus -- its best work still waiting to be done!

About the best he can do now is pivot and then to see if
he's still on the trail to himself, because so far he's only

caught strangers using it, but how close to himself, how
distant; only a guess -- doesn't want to get too close to the
inhuman darkness these familiar strangers are said to possess!
....

And, he reminds himself, it still might be her, she swore
she would always have his back and what better way
than coming back, and if it's not her... no, he can't
fathom even an inhumanely dark stranger doing that to him!

Which raises the question (had to be somewhere and
it's getting pretty late in the poem so) of whether thinking

will continue at world's end which all depends, as he
sees it, on whether it will ever complete its conception

of what is uniquely... now, or will, thinking, realizing
its many, many mistakes, (and that would take some real
thinking) simply disappear under evolution's relentless plow?

And standing here by the river murmuring its ceaseless
and always senseless homilies, things do look forlorn,

like coming upon a pile of peelings when it was cores he'd
been looking for, and for so long. How important then

must be "looking forward to" in light of creation being so
hard to tell apart from just random happening. Therefore,
living but once one automatically acquires a much wider
perspective on what is viewed; there is no distance that

does not contain the implications of near, though it can't
be reached from here, lacking both a front and a rear.

The idea may be diamond but will it be able to cut, and
accurately, the liquid crystal of time, or be cut in its turn

so it reflects each moment from a multi-faceted point

of view in which his actions are projected in numerous

simultaneous tenses, exploiting the vanishing points
of each, a cubism so fluid it's lost all connection with
even the most radical forms of space-time geometry?

He sees a wall of bicep photos, all of them flexed and
straining but with nothing for them to lift, and knowing

nothing is the hardest thing to get a grip on, let alone
move from its place, and thinking thus he finally sees

how any act, even a supposed, even an imaginary, one
brings nothing itself all the way into a fictional center

where might-have is waiting and... after all, why not --
should it not then triumph in both the most minor and
most major and/or imaginary encounters – for nothing is

a war already... won. The series may remain too incomplete
as yet to choose between cold probability and warm
mystery but choose he must so his life can overcome,
though perhaps but briefly, unrelenting death-driven need.

The Sensation Was Of Sinking Without Going Down

The day brightened, as if digesting the dark, turning
it into fuel; yet it rode the calm sea like a glazed layer
of shadow, outlining odd aspects of landscapes he
could find no particular reason he was being given to see.

He tried to pry himself from this image but it seemed
to be pledged to his cause; his mind, unable to respond,

let the road act as his argument; a familiar desire,
never too long, that is, so it never feels quite long
enough when one reaches the end: a true desire, or

in brief: an object that depends on nothing – outside
of faith. Nothing, that is, when multiplied infinitely.
....
He found himself humming to himself, quite proud
of that conclusion it would seem as he was humming
with the hushed notes the sea leaves on the beach.

Thus buffered from distractions of songbirds and
swishing fronds but included in their presence there

till he felt this layer of being envelop him; imagined
he saw scribbled on its underside the structure of that
day's philosophy, but as seen by clouds, sea currents,

and sand whimsically adding further final touches to
dunes, but in a form he might one day understand more
deeply -- perhaps enough he might even learn to teach?

Thinking thus, he arrived at a place revelers had recently
been, and looking back saw the road moving away,

straighter than he would have thought, as if deciding
his desire was leading it nowhere it wanted to either go
or be. Of course it was headed nowhere as well but...

but what? It had no desire to get anywhere so nowhere
would do nicely, for desire is image-ridden, a compounding
of...desirable (what else?) effects but so subtly interwoven
one has no feeling of being led, like a road but one...

anticipating where it was headed and despite knowing
expectation is always suspect. Like the road image itself...

anyway, the point, and the one he tends to forget, is
that all the while he's been moving on and not at all
like the road because he's never been there before – so

that should take care of that! And since, philosophically
again, it's where he's never been, he's naturally startled
to find himself back at the annual Asylum Fair once more:

birthday suits in banana-shaped jars, vendors with bags
of squeals, endless lines of hawkers offering the first

of theirs in exchange for the last of yours, though the
one they can't remember and the other hasn't happened yet.

And with a few philosophical gymnastics he's able to
convince himself he's never been here before, that the
mad are like a river, can never step into the same madness
twice though being madness it never varies either...put

another way, what's on sale are virtual tickets to games
of chance where a chance is the only prize; not another way,
admittedly, but it will still lead nowhere – most assuredly!
....
And he felt a freedom among them as nowhere else
(he knew he would find it here and without mental
gymnastics either!) and wondered if this unanchored

feeling always led to insanity or like an elixir... might
lead finally beyond it, to the heights of an epic poem or

(it is mad after all), might be setting him up for a lethal
tumble down the imaginary stairs he was making his way up.

Not worth the thought for it was much the same, indeed
almost identical, as when he slowly moved the dial
and voices faint and/or hysterical called out for his

attention but he ignored these pitiful, yet irritating calls
and just kept turning the dial absorbing the voices as if
they were... sensations emanating from within a market
where fruit, fish and game barter for customers while he

felt them all and bought nothing, but... nothing at all!
Madness, trumped without a card in his hand – and they
would certainly understand that! And yet as he moved

away, went back to getting nowhere, if this actually was
the way...anyway, he felt like he'd missed the point,

and though it was nothing like a lover's rejection, just
a cold streamer of air, one dawn might leave behind,

when it was invigorating not imbued with a malicious

chill, when it was sharp but gentle, a laser let's say and
not a spear. And as if to make his point by making its

point, the sun began shaving slivers of light from the
clouds and he shivered to see how thin, and keen,
bright can become! And all the while the market kept

revolving around him, and even though he felt he was
moving nowhere's way... not like being in two places

at once, not exactly: more like being here and going
back -- to make sure he was coming too. So, in those
circumstances it was only natural, to imagine he was

also between the two, riding wind fur like a flea, doing
nothing that came with a future but using now with the

same focus and intensity in order to catch the flares in
his mindscapes, like those from the sun that often disrupt

communications but are never seen by the naked eye, to
use them to get inside the patterns guarding that music
and find the real reason, create it if it can't be located there.

Bumped along on distorted echoes, gaining momentum,
and then... sailing off a cliff watching light dance over the
water like fingers in an exquisite gamelan orchestra... a
vision without any sense of sight till fishermen appeared,

brought the "vision", down to the earth, or rather down to sea
where something besides himself was bound to be worth catching!

Silently they pushed their caique into the sea. Figures straight
from Fayyum but ones who skipped the part where the

stage directions said "here you must die". Looking as if
they'd been rained on for years and that it was raining then.

They paused at the edge of the enormous bay which opened
before them in full frontality, as if reflecting again on how

they got there and then heaved the boat into the bay's wide-
spread legs, started up the engine, the thud slowly increasing
the speed of its rhythm as it converted the chop of the waves

off the sides of the boat into valves, working hard as the bay's
old, but aroused and yearning heart. He wished he could see his
face watching them, share that with the rest of him rooted there!

Thoughts waved their tentacles to impress, or distract him,
but he was in the mood to spot the inner octopus, the place

where it lies secure in its unconscious ink. And by then
the fishermen had moved out to sea and like that!
disappeared as fast as a life at its end, seen in retrospect.
Or so he felt, never having been there yet. Obviously!

Anyway, it did make him feel like a leaf on the spinning
tree of this galaxy deciding the force of the spin would
hold him and he'd never fall; but then insects swept past

like a mockery of his "leaves"; though both were now
more like a swarm of periods hearing of an incomplete

text – no way they were missing that! How bright it still
was as he followed them imagining them pulling melodic
strands from him as from a spider, so bright he could see
the pores in the strands clear and unique as the words he

was thinking of putting in lines, maybe these, maybe not,
words clear in his mind but nameless yet... but that's not

the point which is: that incredible sensation of sinking into
the web he was made to make, but both already there,
so there was a sinking feeling but nothing going....down.

None Of What He Was Given Will Ever Be His Even Once, Let Alone Again

A loud quack falls from wind-smacked leaves.
Ravaged feathers and quills tell a tale
fit only for a ditch while morning's prattle begins again,

always the same no matter the seasons –as if
there were so much else going on
he wouldn't believe…, fussing with
the light, forced to start from the beginning again;

and he knows some of it must be can't-do-without passwords
but so far has no idea if they're the
ones that would make this part of the puzzle
accessible to him or the ones that have
co-opted the puzzle themselves – and for themselves..
....
Could be, but the sky remains glazed the palest of blues,
and is glistening, as if kiln-fresh. Hard to
imagine that just an hour ago, it was a dark, star-
studded mass! Insects rising to meet
the heat could be seen as approximations
of where the stars would be if they had a choice

that is, if he were in desperate need of an outrageous
metaphor and no other one available
understood the work involved.
....
He sets aside his pole and packet of homemade flies.
Not the time to go fishing, obviously.
Could riots in distant slums be
reverberating in insect buzz out here?

And if so (or not so, too early to tell which so and so,
hah!) are all these little intimate adjustments
not only going to at last lead him to
those long-dreamed of consummate arms,
or only once again to go nowhere but into the pile
of self-help memos he's been meaning to
destroy but is letting time recycle like it does all dead stuff.

How will his true self, then, ever get clear, be allowed
to appear when events and his own
emotions continue to interfere? If he had
a friend close enough to understand all this and
he then tried to make him see –
he thinks he'd need to find another friend, indeed.

And even if he were fishing he wouldn't be fishing for
much more than that, and even then,
while watching simultaneously some hidden
tree shedding scale-like petals and for
some reason he remembers the day
when they found her by her pool scrubbing
dollar bills with Astroturf.

Could there be a good reason for asking why, now, when
no one could come up with one back then?
And did the bank replace the bills
or get her turfed out of her job to settle the bill.

And what of the nights he spent in alleys watching the
small wind of decay lapping up drool
from a wino's lips? But then no one there
had lived with himself in so long
that they would have died if a meeting had

occurred then. Passing out removed
the chance of it just passing by.

One of those times when things seem, somehow, to
just... appear: but why does it almost
inevitably tend to be road-kill or a dumpster filling
up? So he can learn what it feels like to be treated as

if he were a toxic spill? That's like teaching the blind to be
blind (but not the seeing to see – there's always
something to learn there – try it, you'll see!)
There's a book on the subject or so he's heard:
A Guide to Hidden Communities, How and Where They Can Be
Found.

Or could have been. The book is long out of print and anyway the
communities weren't so much
hidden as gone away... out of sight out of mind
so to speak. And though survival alone
might suffice as incontrovertible evidence of them –
it can't be introduced as an explanation or
excuse for an act, as it so often is. And since they
didn't survive... finding does not mean finding in time..
....
Cranes dip and swoop in the distance, delicately as dancers
challenging the notion large motions lead to
the berserk. Shrieks, squeals, thuds in
profusion moving silence out of this dead-end
part of town; the air is blue, brittle,
metallic, even a kitten's mew here hurts.

An old woman shuffles past and asks him if he's "got a night?"
He gives her a cupped firefly without thinking

and a tear comes into her eyes ---
and wouldn't you know: the exact same shape!

(Considering how tenuous our grip on anything, it's a
miracle experience lasts long enough for
even an idea of it to form, let alone
then being held responsible for being the
cause all this... stuff.) If he assumes it makes sense

he's living and for some reason knows he is.... well, that's
about it. But when the lake of his time is finally
drained who will be the seer able to read his bones,
that is, find them first in the mud and then prove
them to be ...identifiably his? And while he's on it, if
a clone could be made from the marrow would it
know in a completely different way what it meant to die?
Or any way at all? He doesn't so why would his clone?

And his mind unable to leave the topic alone, makes him
wonder if the Resurrection also has that same
factor of insecurity to deal with, the constant fear
there's been some mistake? Can't help
but wonder, that is, if wonder isn't the real mistake!
      ....
But if love is to prevail in the end, then the end may not
be as near as some think; visions of Melusine
and Raimondin, scientifically enhanced by now,
using dawn's misty embroideries instead
of trysts, not to swoon in or on but to rub like
ointment over new but still raw and inflamed tattoos!
Thinking that while standing just outside
the kitchen watching flapjacks somersaulting as
if putting off the inevitable. Or till rain can begin to fall

like a dithyramb coming apart and from under an awning
he observes men leaning over a gushing
sewer as if trying to get high though anyone could
see it was too early yet for a real bacchanal.
The longer he looks the deeper they seem to bend –
because the gusher has acquired a halo and sounds like a prayer?

He's hungry but the flapjacks never seem to tire of their
tedious antics and the inevitable, though it
contains all things, is inedible so he imagines
himself as the winder of wind but in a way that others
would see him with the stature of a
magnificent tree that bats this wind from
limb to limb, then using the tattered rags for… repairs.

For now it seems a pleasing, if not convincing, way to
explain why none of what he was
given will ever be his even once, let alone again.

A Valley, A Village, And Pretty Much Take It From There

Furious disconnect of dawn soundlessly shattering
the deepest links of night. Mountains rear
up as if fast-forwarding to the Deeper History of Time.

The scene then settles so quickly it's indistinguishable
from the recent past, while shadows
work the dead zones of his waking mind as if it

might never wake, focusing a light as intense as martyrdom
on them, though the words maintain everything,
including everyone, is doing just fine.
....
Next thing he knows he's standing at the end of a valley,
which end he can't say, where nearly everything,
including everyone again, will always
be looking down on him, where, perhaps in anticipation
the grey light is unrolling its frost-stiff carpet

while the village, hidden in there can be heard shifting
stiffly, as if trying to smooth out its hardening
chronological wrinkles. A cold but
somehow erotic fog (its pre-coital texture perhaps?)

is patchily dampening the autumn orchard where the carpet
stops. How readily he imagines the form of
Aphrodite wandering through the trees, nibbling
on a peach, licking up the juice, feeling it
welling, as if willing itself to become part of her lips!
....
Later. Elsewhere. In that sequence a man of habit he

remains, the light now at glacier depth
on this side of the mountain and the dark
enveloped inside it is shaped like a candle tipped
by the flame of morning as if the muse
has somehow been coaxed inside.

And so the moments whine on in his head as if they were
coffee beans being ground; but he knows his
thought better than that, it's pepper with a touch of
gunpowder and when it's fine enough,
he thinks, he might sprinkle some on this paper,

see if a hidden message is brought up, or at least be given
another chance at deciphering what blank
itself is trying to articulate – it got as far
as paper, he must assume it wants to go all the way!
One of these days, he swears, he's going
to blow both of them up – and gets the vague
idea he also hears this one saying "me too!"
....
And it would be time for coffee, if he were home, and
indeed, it would already ground and nearly
made: Balkan, gritty and as unsweetened
as the "sweet nothings" she whispered in passing –
till the passing passed with the whisper,
took so long, long in the no-time-at-all sense –
and even when it did come back it was
as an always more garbled version of farewell?

Back in the days when he still shaved but was always
unshaven, stubble as coarse as that coffee
and there was her delicate face rubbing against
his whiskers as if challenging them to

soften up and they did or so he felt, give way,

anyway, to the whispers and the depth of meaning
her whispering then implied – a depth of
being is how he sees it now and now knows he
knew even then – but who was to know how deep being went?

So the steam of dissipating fog now seems to be rising,
but not as if toward the light, but as if
the light were boosting it up to the sky and
that the light itself was always getting a boost from
the earth's own natural, always fermenting brew.

When he sees it like that it does seem natural – the landscape
so willing to go along with what is surely
an untenable view of the process – as if "you
never know" was the way evolution
managed to do what no one has ever been
able to guess and still can't now.   Nonetheless feeling…

bolstered and by no more than considering his whimsical
take on the morning as one deeply ingrained
in reality, the feeling growing as he
moves further and further up the valley, toward
the other end that doesn't end, merely
becomes a plain…and a plain one at that!

Anyway watching as he moves along the mist being boosted,
apparently in no hurry to rise on its own,
gathered into what could be robed figures, like
one sees in choirs and his memory starts looking
for the heights such choirs imply and,
as always, fails; and the image immediately falls apart

whatever it was, or is, or might have been if… too mystic
in any case to contain the bubbling, bursting
moment, never choiring but choking on its own
scream –with all its paper, pens, religions,
cement, steel, bombs, and flies, flies, flies! and
none of these can ever encompass
the silent sifting down of the light of time

(and does it never come down to rise?) till it's so fine it
can only be compared to dark! Or could be
if one didn't, and right that moment, run out of time.
      ....
The departing mist has returned the village intact, just
soft enough he knows it's never dry or
ever lacking in that nameless ingredient that
keeps it moist and radiant. So if he gets a shock from

touching anything it won't be like the one the desert's so
famed for: but far slower, more elaborate;
no sparks; no light flare of surprise: no surprise
at all. A soundless bell struck. Nothing to
be surprised about. Here at this point of the valley, itself

at an abnormal height, he finds himself looking at the
dim cleft suffused with an organic pink and
wishes again he had just once seen the
light of the womb before he left.
Knew what it meant when it was his alone,
and if it tried to hold onto his shape after he was gone,

and for how long. At all? Or did he, like a true child of God,
assume he was the light being let out,

the rosy dawn of a new world! Even the finest
windows wouldn't know if this
happened to be the light they were now letting in.
．．．．．．．．．．．．．．．．．．．．．．．．．．．．．．．．．．．．
Beyond, the sky turns such an intense blue it seems like a
warning: this is God's skin, His largest organ too,
the way he reaches the feel of all worlds
simultaneously. In effect, it covers nothing and even
that's a stretch. And if its surface held
fingerprints would he, or He for that matter,
want to be one of the ones identified by them?

The words are with him but he's yet to find a perfect
match to any idea he (they) may be trying to
express, for most words are alibis or aliases or
merely disguised and/or ambiguously covered blanks.

So the poem must survive, if at all, like the village in
the valley, by setting moments in guesswork
order that fit but not always a discriminatingly
fickle mind. A valley, a village and pretty much take it
form there. Exactly the same way nature treats all
its hypotheses: presenting them as incontrovertible fact .

A Dance Best Attempted By Those Long Experienced At Being Amateurs

He's sheathed in morning, tight as skin, and like skin
permeated by the senses moving in and
out of it; so what impinges, leaves

echoes, and they accrete; an ambiance reserved
for only the most private memories.

Morning light pinging as if looking for unexplored,
and mellifluously sonorous, discrepancies in depth.

Brief tingle of ozone; like the air stirred at the tip
of a snapped whip – too much of somewhere
else spilled into here, not ready for it yet.

He can barely remember when he used to feel...
spacious, regularly spent a day trying to
fill himself up, giggling at how much he held...!

while now his time seems to be increasingly spent
in new, and ingenious, ways to just get into and

out of himself. Strenuous but no longer intimate.
He assumes the sky still burnishes dawn with its

former care but his focus is no longer stable and even
when it is, he's no longer able, somehow, to share.

He knows a moment may be big as a mountain, just as
he knows the needle point of the pinnacle is what

really counts and he also knows the mind must find
a balance equally as... rarefied... but how long can

one be expected to maintain an organic equilibrium
when unpredictability remains the core of the living game?

Horizons dissolve as if being withdrawn from circulation...
if he hasn't fathomed them by now, then... why can't

he remember the sky-shelves are restocked every day?
Why can't he learn that seeing what is before him
is neither seeing nor remembering but forgetting,

trying to cover its tracks! Not to worry, he tells himself,
for clouds are bobbing in a calm sky like boats in a calm
sea. The window's flaws make birds flying past look

urgent -- to prove they're exceptions to even these
most flexible of rules? Lurk is with him here, long

enough anyway to compare what he's spotted in hiding,
if not where. Not to be remembered as such but more
for the inspiration of the spur-of-the-moment snatching

up that one vital dot among all the rest, so exquisite so...
falconesque? Left on its own, each thing imagined,

he's come to believe, is driven to outdo all others, till
it inevitably would become grotesque – if art didn't put
it to the test -- which it always, but gloriously, fails!

Then, before he's made to put that to the test and while
ancient terraces are getting ready to escort the moon

down to the harbor where tourists have gathered and who
will only use it to stultify the cartoon they're drawing
of themselves while making a hash of a local dance,

anyway, then he will descend, right behind that moon, and
dancing in his own way to the rhythm of beams the moon
releases then -- coming on, going out, one by one...always

maintaining their distance; while holding each focus close: --
a dance best attempted by those experienced at being amateurs.

From A Distance Mistakes Can Often Be Mistaken For Right Ways

Morning so still it could have been a single moment –
one not consummated -- waiting for the grand
inflation of now! And so, he hardly dared breathe,
afraid of collapsing, destroying this singular
state, to the point even the trees seem beset by
the same anxiety as his, but even deeper in thrall to

an ultra-sensitive state of spring... till one shingle slipped
off the roof and crashed, as if tired of doing
nothing, though that was more or less the reason
why it was there. But then things always turn
out differently than he expects; so how, when,
will he know what deserves, at least, his true respect?
....
The wind then gave one of its mad bony laughs and the
trees broke out of their trance and merely by
gaining momentum, escaping what they had been,
and becoming what they were meant to be:
not just always stretching upward but reweaving
light and shadow over and over so whether bare or
full-leaved their presence was always enhanced
by a chance at strobic surprise. So even clouds, once

exposed to this ambience, took on a certain flamboyancy,
flinging off Medusa-like spirals of turbulence,
edged in polychrome flame though the
light reaching here was still winter-drained, looking
peaked...and the memories he needed then
were still a long way from thawing out
and while the crust was dissolving – it seemed

it was over a seeping wound. This was also the time
he was most likely to mistake tears for
that special blur of desire in a lover's eyes. Well!
   ....

Signs auspicious or otherwise, birds will soon arrive
in a confusion of chatter and trill, acting
quite hysterically as if they'd never
built a nest before, and their slapdash efforts
did look more like homeless shanties than cribs,
though when viewed more carefully
show a clever use of braided winter debris,
and perhaps that's why he finds something
both expired and talismanic in each nest, a harbinger
of what was coming, despair at it's coming here.
   ....

Not that he wouldn't like to form nest-like alliances
between his pen and this debris but the thwack
of a tennis ball off a racket distracts him,
especially when it's then swiftly followed by:
sounds of clouds swelling with rain
sounds of rainbows swept by leaves
sounds of departure gaining speed
sounds of age teetering on the edge of a dying cataract
sounds of laughter as it bobs in a sea's turbulent vat
sounds of harm being done, of desperation,
sounds of merely – somewhere else, the unbridgeable separation.
Sounds of the ceremonial removal of lingerie. Must all
sounds always be burrowing into any and all silence found?

And then he found that he was pulling down the flaps on
his hunting cap over and over again and to
distract himself from such compulsions
tried to think of ways he might still come up

with positive metaphors to express a gun's terrible
and barely suppressed rage. Making the whump! of his heart

unexpectedly soothing, almost like that of the gently pulsing
shadows he once thought of importing, those long
seasoned within the many discrete layers
of dead seas, insinuated into the sand and then...
and then, perhaps, finding they were
endangered, try to find out why the world no longer
seemed to be looking as directly at him as it

once did-- how dispassionately passionate he now would say!
so like how one looks at a piece of a puzzle
as it disappears once fit in, how it
can zoom to monstrous proportions when the
fit is denied. The feel is (was, it seems
now) as if he had learned something from
that look about all of us -- that while of the essence
it has nothing to do with what we found
ourselves in: the look that says: "are you sure?"
when knowing you're not, or rather shouldn't be.

Has to do with the "I" he's concluded, temporarily: so
succinct in itself, so sure, not needing
another letter of help but...nonetheless when
considered in relation to "itself", to "him" this "I"
feels as if it were one of countless echoing
sounds, like "om" but even more desperate, scattered
about in thoughts and senses as yet unclaimed. Or something

like that. Just as the pulse of the heart may indeed be
more overwhelming than the pulse of the sun,
so the "I" is far more overpowering than

any "me" and neither of these revelations are
for everyone – and so enforced anonymity. And thus
may also be why the "I" is always trying to
change the rules of the game, and just as the "me"
starts to play, that is, to, in effect, preclude it being a game.
....
The surf on which morning was poured was grey and
hard; liquid granite. But now it's dark, and
so the surf is of a consistency that seems
to depend on what part of the unknown one wants
to feel it's conforming to. This metaphysical
weave to his thought must have also been part of
the comfort blanket in his crib – so when,
seems logical, the nipple was removed he didn't die
of shock but was immediately... sucked into a greater reality.

Just one of the many inscrutable ways he somehow came
to know the tap on the womb-sanctum is never
fully turned off. And if that seems a little
too...too, then at the very least it could explain
our knack for meditation, without any guru
needed, the thirst to again experience the world
from which all our ideas about anything have not yet been
thought though obviously, as well, have not
been erased as he's thinking them – what could be
closer to the womb experience, as it was getting us ready

for rude reality anyway, but making sure all the really
hard parts were saved for later... till now it's
just a conceptual womb, to which one can
retreat till he feels like an utter stranger
to himself, as he once felt when he wasn't and
had no idea of he, a most intimate space where perspectives,

as it were, of selves are imposed on yet other
perspectives of selves, like fists topping one another
in air – but never opening to disclose what's in their palms.

Prime reason, he's come to think, why in aging he's found
its gets harder and harder to tell going ahead from
coming back, harder yet to keep them apart.
He calls it here, others say there, if we split the difference
we arrive at nowhere or, as he prefers,
not anywhere as that's how he feels now at
what out of habit he still calls home. And even
if consciousness is aware of what we are going to do
before we do it, it still knows nothing
of the nature of next because by then it's been
done, is past, everything, or so he's been told,
has read anyway, that is, what's next still comes after
the fact of becoming aware that it is.

....

Houses like stains in the late evening light. Cones of pulsing
illumination, reminiscent of old and beloved states
of taste and touch. Sudden white squares in
the sky like pictures of spatial death, just as lightning's
theatrics begin once again to hold summer in
thrall by their awesomeness, so simple strings of rain,
can perhaps use these… fingers to pluck out his
sound from all the turbulence – and depending on how
acute he is right then to distance, their interpretation
could be taken for either mistakes or mistaken for right ways.

Detachment Or An Active Solitude?

And again the sky darkening, seeming to cloud his senses
as well, dimming the light of insight not from without but
from within. While outside his perception is distracted by
those insect-like black dots in his eyes dancing about,
each pretending to be a vanishing point so what at his age
should be limelight is closer to citrus zest, though on a
cosmic scale, or is it this coarsest of pulverized fake rubies

evening is readying for him? Other, real lights, pop on here
and there, slowly strengthen like the peaches did on
successive dawns last month. So things could be reenacting
their ontogeny but only after learning they might have
other choices so the crunch of gravel from unseen yards
could as easily be raccoons or mutts or the cozy rattle of leaves,

or even the faint applause of the sea on a pebbled beach –
one where he could imagine Demosthenes pacing, determined
to unknot his speech; briefly invigorating, living vicariously
what's truly in a name, but soon overwhelmed, lost in the
infinite possibilities the future doesn't hold for him anymore.

That is, lost for good. That is, he's undoubtedly had his quotient
of edge-time, felt in its many "sightings" what purports in
the reports of mystics to be the soul coming out of hiding,
to enjoy this world of wonders its so bent on removing us from –

his take anyway, especially after checking on how advanced
his teetering is, its effect on his state of equilibrium, perhaps
even casually adding another scratch to the dark glass of his
being with the diamond (strictly Platonic) of eternity, outline

of a portal, suggested embrace it never works, too childish,

Christ knew what he was talking about when he said we had
to become as little children... it's boring as fairy tales, more
so since all the human-like squirrels and toads have disappeared...
anyway, he becomes quickly bored, as only a true expert on the
exquisite can be; or so he'd like to think and memory seems to
be willing to go to luminous lengths at times like these... on
the other hand these "sightings" do seem to revive his lagging
attachment to that sense of the "exquisite", that it does indeed
hold patents on the enhancements he's done to what he calls "me".
....
That odd vagueness that seems more closely focused than any
detail is or possibly can be, exhilarating but so very tiring,
like concentrating on the womb that nothingness is now
claimed to be. So it's good to turn to the real night, abuzz with
tree frogs patiently chorusing and the strident echoes of the
still wild hopes of his youth strutting its new found strength
in the light of that youth that will admit to no dark, so strong

it feels... not so much absurd as inconceivable and yet memory,
for whatever reason, seems to never want to forget if, and
indeed tends to enrich it to counteract the poverty of age?
Perhaps, and perhaps that's why the darkness has a light he
now finds more suitable, somehow, as if this incredible mix
of his feelings, no longer as intense as they once were, now
need the blind man's touch of the dark to act, as no one

can see them, and it's as if they had resumed their former shape
and vitality, could still turn with ease from ghost-breath
gymnastics to throbbing veins of passion and resounding
fiercely with them as it climbs upward, higher than mountains
dare, never peaking as mountains do, never disappearing into

that mysterious instant that seems to be made of pure height,

a space so private anyway, one can't find it anywhere in the
sky, night or day… no, his climbing would not be toward
but into, each a step on a ladder quite incomparable…and
so on, oh youth, oh memory so lovingly, so willingly duped!
And then, breaking though to real night again, crickets now
having joined in, and then immediately after the fireflies,

as if continuing to practice at star-signaling and not making
much progress, but then maybe the stars aren't really signaling
much, "look at me, how high I'm up in the airless!" things
like that…anyway, exuberant and unflagging allies at least
till the reverie is rudely broken by boom-box frogs themselves
as suddenly silenced by a single bassoon-like note from an
owl; he's heard all of it before, but never all at one time –

or so he thinks every time. However, every time isn't now and
that's not the real point either which is despite the fact of that
felt alliance none of what's calling out seems to be calling to
him, for him he means (and why every time may never be
enough) and despite, or in spite of it anyway, he still feels he
must somehow respond if for no other reason than it's the only
way the darkness inside him may complete its ring around its

world, as the night does around its, both allowing named and
nameless voices to sink within and search for and perhaps even
find their identity – though it be as temporary as each darkness
is, temporary but always returning, and being dark nothing can
penetrate the sense of privacy engendered, stars and thoughts
not signaling but showing themselves to be inviolate, having
compressed all the confusion of light and dark together then and

then mixing them into the haunting lassitude of that barely audible OM that has emerged from the owl's HOO and then stretching it from both ends till OM finally merges with the reality into which we all eventually disappear? Stretched so far that what he finally hears sounds far closer to… HOME. Not that there is any need to look for such resolutions but rather to accept them as but another of one's failures to move out of the world of habit, to make sure beauty always retains desire as its first choice and whether as detachment or an active solitude,

close enough together they can hear the pleading note in each other's unique voice. For now he would limit himself to finding the shell that will tell him all it heard when the sea thought no one was listening. Then be given just enough time, nothing longer than a sigh escaping water on a quiet night would be needed, for the sea to come to him on its own, swirling round like a complex pulse, revealing to him the original design of that still unimaginable desire that eventually led to the human heart.

The Trick Is To Get There Just As It's Turning Away And In Such A Manner You Can Be Sure It Won't Turn Back

The sky suddenly loomed, an enormous abstract craving that
could never be sated, let alone satisfied, with what
it had. It made no sense but felt like a
monastery dug out of a mountain and spread over
the day like prayer; nothing exclusive about it –
could just as well have begun with lightning striking a tree

and the tree then speaking in tongues; now it's all desiccation
and obsession; minds teetering while stretching
trying to find a hold though it may be no
more than touching the tip of the pin the last
angel just left. Part, it seems, of this need to explain
a state so overwhelmingly complex he can
never be an important part of even a part of it.

All the while voracious insects continue to eat July away.
Pyrotechnics of shooting stars turning the sky
into an image of an overheated brain and
the two of them there watching it create something
much larger and more abstract than any kind
of brain would have been capable of thinking of, and
even if it could –would it be amenable to thinking such thoughts?

And all the while horizons are sinking endlessly into
themselves, like layers of the unconscious
performing for the world that's not aware or caring,
if it's horizons or the unconscious performing
out there. But he does feel those layers shifting and
interacting -- most often in the morning while
watching night disappear, imagining them as dust

clouds in which stars are hidden and slowly
cooling or on stormy mornings after turbulent nights
more like the imminent crystallizations of incipient inspirations

and transforming them into insidious intents, kept hidden for the
time being, in those deep marine caves of his
ontogeny – where it also seems one must
go to find all the best kept secrets, best kept because
they're disguised as the greatest lies.

To escape, while not forgetting the lotus-imbued pipedreams
drifting above undulant lagoons, no, remembering
but ignoring them, for all he wants to take
from there are small shocks of non-recognition,
showing there is still a lot of dark to feel his way through.

Then to dry off afterward with the fine threads of the sky's
mineral hair, listening to the rain-barrels gurgling
with digested storm, close to the sound
he's sure the unconscious made when it was
being nurtured in cloud-softened latitudes. Gradually
getting used to a life that would be spent in
cloud-soft shadows, it could shape as it would,
sending these shapes rippling into the light
of our sleep we never see – not as light anyway, but more

as the setting in which the still malleable clay of day-warm
images is molded into what we call dreams
but are really no more than what the day, time-bound,
was unable to say, that is, till these shadows
are, at last, able to thus make their own way into
day and join the other shadows already there, meld into

the waves ripening on the lakes of summer, where dozing
on a beach he finds himself imagining using
them as transfers on his journey to isles still without
bliss but looking as if they had to be next in
line, and feel the exhaustion of night as it lets its
light-years of gathered music fall in jumbled chords
from the sky. The unconscious has been there, done that,

true enough, but never this way before, that it alone knows
the world that was, must also be the world
that will be, but, again, unrecognizable having by then
the time to become what went unrealized not
only in deed, but was not even recognized as being
there – no mystery, no mistakes made; no corrections, just
taking the roads that can still be taken when
the others have been followed all the way to their end.

The self then merely part of what gets done and a part that
is of little help in getting it done it would seem.
Think of it, he thinks, as being like
the pavements that melt and puddle in heat
as reverting to their ancestral tar, then extrapolate
and observe them flowing away filling…
but who's to say what ? It's shocking but not like

the shock, for example, of when he saw a dumpster draped
with a dead tiger, a note affixed; "Sorry,
I thought the zoo was a video arcade!" but
knowing there's a great lake of prescient oil
within him as well (the shock came on
a pavement-melting day, tar, so…) and it fuels
his imagination and takes his creations to vistas that
he could never have dreamed of, but did

dream of, if only as part of a metaphysically altered light!

Of course he doesn't want to leave it at that but chances
are something even more inexplicable
and undoubtedly worse would soon take its place.
Trying to find answers is like taking in
strays – they're happy to have a home till it's
time again to resume their stray. And all the while
the fire of inspiration, like a lunatic Gothic mason, is
carving spires of starting points which then
collapse and must make the rest of their way as ash –

and without one helical turn! Color doesn't matter, any will
do as a symbolic window for what's to
be seen in the unchanging black of blind
solemnity anyway? So why not tear tomorrow off
calendars rather than yesterday? After all,
the past is the only thing we ever made that lasted,
that works in a way… the problem is what
we leave behind takes some time to sort and properly…
dematerialize. One may say poet and think he's said enough,

while another says storm, and likes it rough; he once said
solitude till he was filled by a silence of far
sterner stuff. All of them agreed, in the end, on
a general "me" but then echoes interfered and important
parts of the text, when the echoes ceased, were
found blacked out. And again the sky is so full of
itself he feels at times like these, it will soon
have to fall or move elsewhere! And then there are

the stars with trillions of orbits under their astral belts
and yet not one has proved to be a viable route

out of nothingness – or for that matter into it.
Like white mirrors waiting for black reflections, belief
will never supply the physical evidence,
though of course there are certain tests: use an
avenue as if it were a key, open traffic as
you scribble frantically, first having removed A and D

from your alphabet. See then what her coat does for her
knees! That is, each step depends on light
and air; beware. Cut up a Cezanne print, move
the pieces around till they make a new
kind of sense; the same way time scissors memory,
so we're able to recognize what we have never seen.

A brisk wind then brusquely lifts the heavy dresses of
summer from trees but doesn't seem to
find what it's looking for in the entire well-
attired woods. Who knows, the bark may have a message

and even a bite. And all the while a slow sprinkle of
invisible mist is scratching out the day's text
being written on sand: the day thinks it's
left us something, the sand shows no regrets.
Like asterisks to footnotes – but will they then appear
on tomorrow's page? The wind meanwhile
bursts free of a nightmarishly sticky cloud, glides
like a gull over a frilly sea, races straight up
a cliff, tears a flag from a pinnacle rock, without
distracting, or more likely, detecting him.

Fair enough, for he's lost in thoughts about a centaur
caught with the moon in his hunting
bag, that segues and gets deeply involved

with a reindeer with bad case of mange and then
mutated zebras going insane as their stripes
can't make up their minds on... what?
So rather than looking for meaning to expand its
fief he would search the dark corners of comprehend,
persist at it: someone or something understand –
and understanding, will also know, at least, what that means.

The trick is getting there just as it's turning away and,
in such a manner, you can be sure it won't turn back.

Long Ago: Such A Strange Aesthetic!

Long ago: such a strange aesthetic! Tempests of infancy,
squalls untouched by any age at all but no longer conjoined

to their original course: all those separate graves that had
to be dug, and only after did one try to decide whether

they needed tending or not! Is the day still alive when
it's interred in the night? Grim reminders, vouchers

accepted only by certain moons. Coming back to the keeper
of remainders, his so-far reliable finder; he asks for

nothing more of, for now, than an air kiss from the sun and
a wind that only flashes its teeth. And even if he feels

sure no one has ever furthered himself (the idea itself
ridiculous)he wouldn't want to try going back, which is absurd.

No, everything is lying before him as it always has
and arguing both sides of each thing as if not knowing

they have as many sides as fluctuating dimensions
demand! Belief but a wily lizard sunning himself on

them, but just there long enough to screw up a moment
when knowing was imminent -- then immediately hiding –

in plain sight, why not, who would ever believe he was
looking at belief? Such laments cluster become opaque –

like fog in the eyes; both dissipate but only one ascends
while the other remains somewhere secluded bearing

the steady shudder of an unseen sea – he hears things
falling away, getting closer to his part of the cliff.

But they prove to be no more than a trunk, a greasy
fedora, an overcoat smelling of all the foul weather

it absorbed before it died, and a raincoat that now
looks like it suffered from a terrible drought. Talk about

long ago: he's never felt as adult as he did then, when
putting them on for the first time! And photos of him

dressed like that now seem to be of nothing but patterns
of weeds or reconnaissance photos taken from a great

height. Was he really there, or is this just another lizard-
like cameo appearance of belief? No, for he remembers

they were meant to be select moments, that themselves
were meant to be collector's items, collectibles anyway,

and then when they lost all their value and almost
immediately rather then later, not really wanting to

throw them away and having an attic already jammed,
on the other hand what better place to put things in

than what's already jammed – more the merrier thing.
Concluding they were worth jamming in as they

were keys though in retrospect just putting them there
probably meant the locks had already been changed

and there were no keys to them or were, but the change
came after his reality, when things like that were

never locked, if lost or stolen who cared…anyway!
For him that also seemed the way it was meant to be;

things built up around him and he wasn't so much the
center as deeper and deeper between. And that

papier-mâché moon that crumbled like confetti
when lifted by his horizon arms from the trunk, feeling

as if they had reacquired their once enormous reach.
Silver dust sifting onto his parent's wedding picture

just underneath. And since he never met those people
shown in it, he's not sure what he should feel, if

anything, because there is nothing there that he missed.
So, he'll put it back in the long-ago-is-such-a-strange

-aesthetic chest, not where he found it but on the next
layer of laid-to-rest. What's wrong is these pictures always

show people looking ahead when they're really trying
to look back to then – anyway, there's a fedora and

a raincoat in their picture's background, new looking –
worn there for the first time? When he put them on

they felt not only old but dead, wasted by storm and
drought and he then realized he was wearing the only

legacy he would ever have – and quickly took them off
but held them before him, trying to imagine himself the

person wearing them and wondering if he knew as little about
himself as he seemed to and for his sake hoping that was the case.

On Despair Setting Off On A New Course

Night torrential with shooting stars – all the accusations
made against God by our race? Or his torrid replies?

Or a brain seething with words searching for the
door out of the night it finds itself directionless in?
....
Morning, a muggy surge, heave of a swamp -- seeing
stars as if they were his breath trapped in a plastic bag,

one just being tied. Cranky infant, a slightly septic
smell: last waste of the womb as it's being expelled?

Old folks attending making quieting sounds more for
themselves than the child: remembering, perhaps,

when lullabies fell from their moon too, but also when
that whisper went cold as did the meaning of "soon...soon?"
....
The mother late for her second job, the only one that
pays, has trouble with a zipper, her hair somehow

caught in it and when all of it is finally torn out in
frustration how can she possibly know despair has

set off on a new course? And how can he for that matter
when his street waits as always, these last few endless

days that is, like a predator; too bright, too early, overly
amplified; his senses just go on giving and it's really

not safe to stay unprotected for too long inside himself;
he should, and quickly, search out memory's periscope

holes, before they have time to command "down",
and in any case none offer more than a partial impartial

view even when it's one nothing seems partial to. He
would also keep in mind all the times he stood under a

shedding tree and came away with empty hands. But he
kept moving, this emptiness itself a spur to not hang

around, kept thinking the numinous couldn't have lapsed
yet. After all, he has... must be countless names by now

so if it has, he can pretend, long enough anyway that
someone, somewhere. will remember one of them,

what it referred to, or how wonderful he is, was, and so
what if he never thinks of himself that way or any way now?
....
It's a sure alternative, naming, that is; why "why" can
never be answered by why not. No more confusing than

cats pouncing and then puzzling over the mystery of
fluttering empty air. Is it a warning, or a cautioning look:

that he shouldn't try to determine the destiny of his
dreams too early because then it's inevitable he'll leave

their realization for the ever-lurking "too late". Quite
amazing how much one can read into a wordless look!

Amazing or not, one would be better off choosing, say,
lips that know how to kiss each pastel shade of the mind,

eyes that can look through the hot milk of noon, ears
that can hear pumas brushing against the berries of

silence, legs that can spring from summits, hands that
know where to reach in the void for the hidden holds!
....
Remembering then, finally, in time and who knows…
recalling in any case the rise and fall of his hair in the

wind along the scalloped coastline, the lacy fingers
of foam caressing the rude virility of rock, the hiss

escaping from the thrill of filling tight crevices, and
then, suspended in a world of float, finding himself

embraced in the sigh of high heather: how does one
keep such intimacy safe in a world increasingly intent

on exposing itself and as if it were auditioning for porn?
Thoughts drift off from there, imageless as smoke

does on a windless autumn day, neither able to stop
reshaping themselves, both waiting for the pines to

find the water cached in the tight crevices of shriveled
clouds, as if they were natural dowsing rods, waiting till

the world crackles with the fast helter-skelter flight
of those thoughts, till even the smoke is churned

into a white, butter-like material, hard as ice: clear
as a window but with no view allowed. Like the moon

but far colder, enough, that if night touched it, it might
freeze and shatter, and from nothing more than just fright –

as if its dark side were encroaching on its light one, as
if it were the moon, or the moon as it dreamed it was!
....
Wheat sways in the fields – the impression is of hooded
figures in a medieval harvest pageant. And this, as all

the obvious beauties he's mentioned, and so many more,
he can only see when he's had to suffer his way, gladly

or not, to a view. And from his memories he knows not
to expect them again in the land of no-later; not even

as palimpsest fusions, and never as labels, of course.
For the self-imposed images of art were never meant to

fit the real world but were rather meant to give it a
reason for taking yet another chance, a whisper perhaps:

"it won't always be there so…" so, he wasn't surprised
when he read that a madman's brain looks like vermiculate

stone, a bastion undermined by conspirators who once
securely inside then conspire against themselves, and all

his natural enemies feel safe storming it. Even birds
take advantage though they only sing outside the places

that are being mined. But then probing any of memory's
dimmer chambers one is bound to be amazed by the sheer

number of crudities scrawled on its walls – some that
would clog a toilet or even tear away the stall itself,

divulge the fate of after all, and just when he thought
now could never be too late? What is it about us that hates

the very things that manage, somehow, to love us in spite
of ourselves? And thinking that it's only natural he's hit

by a swamp surge that in rising seems to further thicken
clouds already thick. Just as natural, even more perhaps

as an infant who goes on gurgling and cooing, having
already forgotten the last and most terrible maelstrom of

conception; soon it will reach next and never understand
why there is no after and worse, why it's always implied.
....
And all at the very same time old folks are sorting out the
few things left in their minds, then scattering them behind

at what they must consider to be strategic distances; hoping
to see them from a new perspective, and that if hope works

just this once, to then glimpse the elusive insight that made
them appealing to memory once – or simply making it

easier to find them amid the unstable clutter of their minds
beset by all the unknowns along despair's new course?

Pull The Other One

Night of wind, brittle leaves snapping, breaking through
his stupor, his tired mind muttering "never
knew they were made out of glass" and
then who knows: the land of time-haunted grass
and then this, seeing how far November

had advanced by dawn, mist layered with its chilled
and still unbroken leaves – fragile, more like arboreal schist.

Motors idling, so like this transitional period when night
gives into light but will shadow it throughout
the day, then as if suddenly deciding racing ahead,

trying it seems to warn the streets and they're not about
to be taken for a ride. Then everything falls
to a lower more somber note as mirrors
are adjusted to the empty drive; and is it ever
worth backing up to maintain the illusion of moving ahead?

For an answer there is a burst of crockery against a far
wall, windows filled with desperate shadows
struggling to get out somehow and he wonders –
how can these shadows be so familiar when he's
never seen the people inside making them?
Then silence -- and it will be a while before he knows

if anything's really wrong or the idling just got too close
to the songs that were sung when hope
was so blithely moving them there, before living as

someone else full time became more private than was
expected, till it was almost a secret and not one

they would like to share with anyone else who might turn
out to be themselves before they came there –
it gets complicated when simplicity
insists on veering. Crockery was made,
he imagines, with the idea of clearing such
moments of insanity before they overthrew minds..
....
Paper on the lawn in fogged plastic looks like the
pale remnants of a thunderbolt buried
in that arboreal schist. Normal, though it
wouldn't have been yesterday. He turns to go back

in, for the light suddenly seems to be signing,
fast and insistent: he can read some
forms of illumination but only when slow
and not too abstract. From here, as it changes its

position on his self-devised map, the horizon looks closer,
then closer, and closer... till suddenly it's
past and another, less clear, appears;
how should he be reading that? Doesn't have
time to, doesn't have to anyway as clouds
become visible, as if they were always here, as

surprising as thinking the leaves were of glass and it
feels almost as good as it would to understand.
A blank filled so he can move on to
the next, equally blank and there will be clouds
and there will be dust, that suspended instant of fear
and then there! and the present becoming

pre- or post-, was or will, but always the only synonym
for now. Perhaps one day not even uncertainty
will need to guess. And then he can
imagine a cascade of blanks he never got
round to, coming back, already filled in,
gift of the blue wild fire sky as if
it were sure he would be the one to spread
the news of its powers... everywhere! Finally!
....
And anyway, as he's spent so much time at ancient sites,
for example, he's already heard this, thought
it before he thought of it (especially now
he's learned that's what is... expected there, of him; us)

or felt it, anyway in the threnody of those oh so versatile
shadows, the ones they compose
as they cruise the ruins of temples and
redefine their configurations, their standing
in, or against, the world, while testing

what might survive if forced to adjust to another form
of life after... and could do it and make it look
as if it were tailor-made...before.

Like opening a long-sealed tomb and finding it full of
the noise of things, still pitifully scrambling,
trying to get – away; out: even from there where they can't
be reached – which may be the point.
....
The engines have departed, like a pack of dogs, he thinks,
after a bone, then, trying to embellish
that thought, getting stuck in a tar pit of traffic,

all flesh and no bones…oh well…anyway,
the engines immediately replaced by an influx
of blowers, mowers, jack-hammers and
panting runners hydrating by the numbers, obsessively,
as if raising the odds, and compulsively, before making a bet.

Assuming for no reason they will win as easily as
looking over their shoulders and somehow
(and even to their astonishment) finding
survival is not laid down the same way as bricks
in a house, but more like unconscious maps
of the contractor's worst mistakes.

(which might explain these occasional fits of aluminum
siding, as if worse means better so one
can only hit one's stride when there
is nothing more to stride to, over, across?)

Back to the scribble and desultory musing on the long-
term effects of road rage, aside from
the flutter, putter, stutter that by the end of
the day has drained the fuel of vision from everyone's eyes.

And ahead, as if out of nowhere (God he'd love to get
a glimpse of that place!) there appears a view
of the land as his first kite espied it
and from it learned the basics of how to
hold on because this was the way one got to
nowhere he thinks now but then it was the leaves,
not brittle, made of the most ethereal of clays,
curling on rivers teaching him all that he
needed to know about flow, the sound of music at

the end of the pier, the essence of how to let go. The steps
seem so short in memory but perhaps just
enough to show him... why he can only hit his
stride when there is nothing more to stride to, over, across?
....
Just as here in November how badly depleted the heat
that rose last summer like juice in ripening
fruit, has become and getting more spent each day;
little more than a sticky residue left behind
by flies but acting as if they were genetic markers...

so he can't help but feel whole futures may be being realized
without him, without even passing through,
or glancing at... his scenic review of evolve.

And now in the shadows that survived that holocaust, he
sees even the thinnest, most flimsy of possible
patterns have already been opted for,
secured -- a tracery of lines or vines, little more
meaningful than Alzheimer recollections
but determined to mean something in spite of that,

while there still is some, albeit erratic, chance, and even
among those who, tough and proud of
their memories, aren't able to grasp they've lost
what made them feel like their very own!
The senile jaw clamps down and down – finding no teeth.

And yet it doesn't take a lot of understanding, just
a willingness to admit a masterpiece does not
have a single master, nor is it a piece.
So there's always a treasure unspent each
time he opens his eyes. And each blink, rather

than blank, an affirmation of that, and
perhaps, only that – just as the sea
in all its depth is actually more rise than fall.

And maybe he's lucky the world doesn't get involved,
leaving him the freedom to imagine how he
might fill in the blanks if the moon were
to return his secrets in silver bound. Maybe it
wouldn't take him all the way through but
doesn't arriving here qualify as a start? Pull the
other one – it's what, in these cases, protocol demands.

There Have To Be Places Where No One's To Blame

Gimpy pigeons, like wind-up toys left by the side of
trashcans just in case...he has the bread but crumbs

no longer fall from his fingers; feeling foolish, while
looking askance as everywhere seems to be blocking

his desperate glance; let it pass they tell him; they'll
always be something not to his taste, and maybe it's

true; what did he gain being preoccupied with getting
through, getting past, while the park went upscale; why

then the feeling that it was, somehow, done behind his
back... the way it turned out who's to tell it from

"c'mon, you know"? The thing to remember is when to
forget; time gives and takes away so fast it's as if it

needs the last second back just to pay for the next! Put
simply (suppressing a laugh) the gap between feel and

express gets harder to bridge and with all the power
surges and sudden outages, the treacherous sideways

slips on slope-less terrain – not even the circumstantial
always collapses into circumstance. Put simply while

(releasing the laugh with many a twist) straight ahead
is meant as a lesson in grasping what can't be reached.

....

But then time never observes what happened after it
passed, just let's it proceed as if the real had been

firmed up enough by its passing, caught up in the
metronomic rise and fall of a thread of history being

drawn by time's needle making a endless seam, history
becoming dogma, as some say... no wonder no one

ever learns anything from it!. He means, rather he...
assumes, that though the pigeons are undoubtedly real

they could just as well have been made by someone
who once read Sailing to Byzantium, and possessed of

a little mechanical skill and a droll cast of mind... no,
really it's too ridiculous. But then Yeats had that charge

made against him for years. And academe, for that
matter (why do we always say that when changing the

subject – because it doesn't matter?) he's noticed still
holds on to patches of ivy and moss, all the while steadily

removing the bricks – there was a thought there, once,
but written down it seems of little more use than an ink

blot and couldn't even be interpreted, tested... and how
does one write a blot off. So one keeps busy outsourcing

anxieties, working with modular nodes designed, supposedly,
to increase the carrying capacity of each personal unit

of... time, so the present can, eventually, hold more of...
itself, become at last what both past and future somehow

lack; why that is so, remains a mystery but to be safe,
he's thinking it might be caused by the distraction of

time's incessant, obsessive ticks, so he will try to slowly,
ever so slowly, remove one or two and in much the

same way as the bricks; time tested he thinks what could
be more timely than that – and laughs -- hopelessly!
....
On the other hand, (what happened to the one hand?
Christ!) no one wants to think of anything built in

stages anymore: there is nothing there and then suddenly,
no instantaneously, but before it becomes time,

there's only complete: the in between somehow morphed
through the cyber world to – see how it goes? Who

knows – as long as there's always room beside the pigeons
for the increasing trash! Or when none of that works like

he, for example, wanted it to, he will merely have to dial
a random sequence of numbers and if anyone answers

he'll know who it is and if no one does he'll know who it
was; if it's busy it could only be him. So! So rather that

re-layering his sequences again or listening for the telling
gurgle as things bottom out, or feeling a poignant sorrow

he'll never understand, except the two go together like
blood and marrow, like vein and bone, like thoughts for

that matter (here he goes again!) apparently spontaneously
generated by the mind, then jettisoned to make room

for more and then... the only reason he can think of is it
has to know more but never admitting it's doing that,

needing to in order to make itself feel right at home, as it
were, when it reaches the mindless...no wonder he's come

to prefer rundown saloons! at the tranquil hour, at least,
ones whose mirrors remain grandly ornamented with

nothing but booze, having somehow escaped the strange
wasting disease caused by owning a self; and thinking

thus sees he hasn't changed... fundamentally: it's the
years are dissolute! Like coming out of the other end

of a tunnel he's been secretly digging for ages, (without
aging of course) one the self knows nothing about, finding

little different from when he went in, so there's nothing
to be secretive about, never was, secrets only kept for

the fun of it, the one-upmanship hell of it. Just that simple
without the need to abstract; more like a sea he can be lost

in without needing to save himself because the "tides"
are of his time and built the coastline themselves. For

there have to be places where no one's to blame and
memory can be arrested for trespassing on what was

doing just fine without anything lying ahead to worry about.
Where he could feel his unconscious absorbing his dying

and wonder, without worrying about it, how it will know
when it's had enough. Not really; he just likes to listen to the
sound of him saying it to himself because between the worst

on one hand (it's back! He knew it!) and the best on the other,
where is the hand that balances them to be found, and found, put?

Who Can He Trust To Keep An Eye On His Hovering Breath?

"Memory's barbell puts too much strain on the present's
muscles for him to lift the real weight of time."

When that makes sense he'll know he's run out of his special
varieties of now. Thinking of later too long
means by the time he gets there it will be gone.
A new regimen is needed – what of all that is settling
and must be first touched before it goes down?

Or maybe he should take up extreme swimming instead –
not go with the flow, and while rejecting
the assistance of all those seductive, against the
current devices; making himself into a
whirlpool and then sucking himself into his
uncharted depths. But while doing that, who can he
trust to keep an eye on his hovering breath?

So how does he keep his balance when push and shove
cannot be avoided or voided? It's physics
goddamnit! And how can he give himself space
when he's always stuck in the middle
of everything that covets that space no matter what

it is – the one anyway through which he's taking his time,
moving out; not that anybody really notices…him,
but then if put in a line-up could he pick
himself out? Makes you think. But in a completely

different way than the one used when wasting time
thinking about death, for it's one of the

few things time knows nothing
about and so can be of no help or hindrance,
for that matter, to him. Even if words suddenly
stopped their mad, monstrous chatter that somehow conceals

an exquisite grasp of matters that never matter after all –
unless they ran into each other by chance
in a poem – and only then are of the essence to
someone who will always remain unknown – the confusion

of devolving echoes would only make what they're
trying to tell him harder to understand
so by the time the echoes had fully faded, how
would he remember what he'd been thinking about before them?

Memory does try: it doesn't know it's telling lies but is still
careful to leave gaps for fate to decide on,
who knows – having barely touched on beginnings
and/or ends – for generally speaking they
do not please and yet they speak only the truth!

He sometimes sees it as a torrent easing through a thick-
leaved tree, the rush then further diverted
and muffled by the eaves so by the time it reaches
his ears he will hear only a far off rumble
of the great mortal turbulence that defines us all.

Lacks a fine touch but has the touché of distance
going for it, disassembled in such a way
its dots can never be rejoined –if intelligence
is to remain the main criterion anyway.

He could say, having said that, that memory deals only

in the hypothetical as it has no idea who
he might have become or what he
even was for that matter that led and left
him here – as it has always been a reaction to

conditions, not an instigator of them. Momentary sensations
that have no idea what they are trying to
describe but know that a lifetime is
less than a hand extended, and a tightly closed
one at that. Faiths churn past chasing down predictions

that got away, under a sky the color of blowing sand.
Caught in traffic's slow avalanche he
wonders if death is like breaking
through to a stretch of straight, open road
or becoming caught in complete gridlock, or just

stalled in the middle of nowhere, more or less like he is now.
For moments in any dimension are like
half-lives, disappear as they happen
and yet take forever doing it, though supposedly
in ever shortening strides till the dark comes
back so thick and heavy even wind can't get through.

One of those afternoons when it gets dark before it
gets dark and then brighter when it
should be quite dark (snow seemingly
comes equipped with its own light and time);
it clears, the darkness falls like a curtain
at the end of a play to be as quickly upstaged by

the moon making the landscape glow as if it were day with
the essence removed, till it too sinks; all

examples of this momentary sensation of later,
used as an identity, as identity itself for that matter

and so is now the true meaning of what this day was about,
though he finds dark is far more obsessive
about itself and far less involved with
his experience than it used to be. He's not sure
he knows that, just sure he really doesn't
want to; an old man has more urgent
things to deal with than sharing with everyone
his experiences of being hopelessly undermined by not.

Fomite

About Fomite

A fomite is a medium capable of transmitting infectious organisms from one individual to another.

"The activity of art is based on the capacity of people to be infected by the feelings of others." Tolstoy, *What Is Art?*

Writing a review on Amazon, Good Reads, Shelfari, Library Thing or other social media sites for readers will help the progress of independent publishing. To submit a review, go to the book page on any of the sites and follow the links for reviews. Books from independent presses rely on reader to reader communications.

For more information or to order any of our books, visit http://www.fomitepress.com/FOMITE/Our_Books.html

More Titles from Fomite...

Novels
Joshua Amses — *During This, Our Nadir*
Joshua Amses — *Raven or Crow*
Joshua Amses — *The Moment Before an Injury*
Jaysinh Birjepatel — *The Good Muslim of Jackson Heights*
Jaysinh Birjepatel — *Nothing Beside Remains*
David Brizer — *Victor Rand*
Paula Closson Buck — *Summer on the Cold War Planet*
Dan Chodorkoff — *Loisaida*
David Adams Cleveland — *Time's Betrayal*
Jaimee Wriston Colbert — *Vanishing Acts*
Roger Coleman — *Skywreck Afternoons*
Marc Estrin — *Hyde*
Marc Estrin — *Kafka's Roach*
Marc Estrin — *Speckled Vanities*
Zdravka Evtimova — *In the Town of Joy and Peace*
Zdravka Evtimova — *Sinfonia Bulgarica*
Daniel Forbes — *Derail This Train Wreck*
Greg Guma — *Dons of Time*
Richard Hawley — *The Three Lives of Jonathan Force*

Fomite

Lamar Herrin — *Father Figure*
Michael Horner — *Damage Control*
Ron Jacobs — *All the Sinners Saints*
Ron Jacobs — *Short Order Frame Up*
Ron Jacobs — *The Co-conspirator's Tale*
Scott Archer Jones — *A Rising Tide of People Swept Away*
Julie Justicz — *A Boy Called Home*
Maggie Kast — *A Free Unsullied Land*
Darrell Kastin — *Shadowboxing with Bukowski*
Coleen Kearon — *Feminist on Fire*
Coleen Kearon — *#triggerwarning*
Jan Englis Leary — *Thicker Than Blood*
Diane Lefer — *Confessions of a Carnivore*
Rob Lenihan — *Born Speaking Lies*
Colin Mitchell — *Roadman*
Ilan Mochari — *Zinsky the Obscure*
Peter Nash — *Parsimony*
Peter Nash — *The Perfection of Things*
Gregory Papadoyiannis — *The Baby Jazz*
Andy Potok — *My Father's Keeper*
Kathryn Roberts — *Companion Plants*
Robert Rosenberg — *Isles of the Blind*
Fred Russell — *Rafi's World*
Ron Savage — *Voyeur in Tangier*
David Schein — *The Adoption*
Lynn Sloan — *Principles of Navigation*
L.E. Smith — *The Consequence of Gesture*
L.E. Smith — *Travers' Inferno*
L.E. Smith — *Untimely RIPped*
Bob Sommer — *A Great Fullness*
Tom Walker — *A Day in the Life*
Susan V. Weiss — *My God, What Have We Done?*
Peter M. Wheelwright — *As It Is On Earth*
Suzie Wizowaty — *The Return of Jason Green*

Poetry
Anna Blackmer — *Hexagrams*
Antonello Borra — *Alfabestiario*
Antonello Borra — *AlphaBetaBestiaro*
Sue Burton — *Little Steel*
David Cavanagh — *Cycling in Plato's Cave*

Fomite

James Connolly — *Picking Up the Bodies*
Greg Delanty — *Loosestrife*
Mason Drukman — *Drawing on Life*
J. C. Ellefson — *Foreign Tales of Exemplum and Woe*
Tina Escaja — *Caida Libre/Free Fall*
Anna Faktorovich — *Improvisational Arguments*
Barry Goldensohn — *Snake in the Spine, Wolf in the Heart*
Barry Goldensohn — *The Hundred Yard Dash Man*
Barry Goldensohn — *The Listener Aspires to the Condition of Music*
R. L. Green — *When — You Remember Deir Yassin*
Kate Magill — *Roadworthy Creature, Roadworthy Craft*
Tony Magistrale — *Entanglements*
Andreas Nolte — *Mascha: The Poems of Mascha Kaléko*
Sherry Olson — *Four-Way Stop*
David Polk — *Drinking the River*
Phliip Ramp — *The Melancholy Of A Life As The Joy Of Living It Slowly Chills*
Janice Miller Potter — *Meanwell*
Joseph D. Reich — *Connecting the Dots to Shangrila*
Joseph D. Reich — *The Hole That Runs Through Utopia*
Joseph D. Reich — *The Housing Market*
Joseph D. Reich — *The Derivation of Cowboys and Indians*
Kennet Rosen and Richard Wilson — *Gomorrah*
Fred Rosenblum — *Vietnumb*
David Schein — *My Murder and Other Local News*
Harold Schweizer — *Miriam's Book*
Scott T. Starbuck — *Industrial Oz*
Scott T. Starbuck — *Hawk on Wire*
Seth Steinzor — *Among the Lost*
Seth Steinzor — *To Join the Lost*
Susan Thomas — *The Empty Notebook Interrogates Itself*
Susan Thomas — *In the Sadness Museum*
Paolo Valesio and Todd Portnowitz — *Midnight in Spoleto*
Sharon Webster — *Everyone Lives Here*
Tony Whedon — *The Tres Riches Heures*
Tony Whedon — *The Falkland Quartet*
Claire Zoghb — *Dispatches from Everest*

Stories
Jay Boyer — *Flight*
Michael Cocchiarale — *Still Time*
Michael Cocchiarale — *Here Is Ware*

Fomite

Neil Connelly — *In the Wake of Our Vows*
Catherine Zobal Dent — *Unfinished Stories of Girls*
Zdravka Evtimova — *Carts and Other Stories*
John Michael Flynn — *Off to the Next Wherever*
Derek Furr — *Semitones*
Derek Furr — *Suite for Three Voices*
Elizabeth Genovise — *Where There Are Two or More*
Andrei Guriuanu — *Body of Work*
Zeke Jarvis — *In A Family Way*
Jan Englis Leary — *Skating on the Vertical*
Marjorie Maddox — *What She Was Saying*
William Marquess — *Boom-shacka-lacka*
Gary Miller — *Museum of the Americas*
Jennifer Anne Moses — *Visiting Hours*
Martin Ott — *Interrogations*
Jack Pulaski — *Love's Labours*
Charles Rafferty — *Saturday Night at Magellan's*
Ron Savage — *What We Do For Love*
Fred Skolnik— *Americans and Other Stories*
Lynn Sloan — *This Far Isn't Far Enough*
L.E. Smith — *Views Cost Extra*
Caitlin Hamilton Summie — *To Lay To Rest Our Ghosts*
Susan Thomas — *Among Angelic Orders*
Tom Walker — *Signed Confessions*
Silas Dent Zobal — *The Inconvenience of the Wings*

Odd Birds
Micheal Breiner — *the way none of this happened*
J. C. Ellefson — *Under the Influence*
David Ross Gunn — *Cautionary Chronicles*
Andrei Guriuanu — *The Darkest City*
Gail Holst-Warhaft — *The Fall of Athens*
Roger Leboitz — *A Guide to the Western Slopes and the Outlying Area*
dug Nap— *Artsy Fartsy*
Delia Bell Robinson — *A Shirtwaist Story*
Peter Schumann — *Bread & Sentences*
Peter Schumann — *Charlotte Salomon*
Peter Schumann — *Faust 3*
Peter Schumann — *Planet Kasper, Volumes One and Two*
Peter Schumann — *We*

Fomite

Plays
Stephen Goldberg — *Screwed and Other Plays*
Michele Markarian — *Unborn Children of America*

Essays
Robert Sommer — *Losing Francis: Essays on the Wars at Home*

Fomite

www.ingramcontent.com/pod-product-compliance
Lightning Source LLC
Chambersburg PA
CBHW021441080526
44588CB00009B/630